PR
1

By
EAMONN G. MONGEY, D.P.A.,
BARRISTER-AT-LAW,

Former Assistant Probate Officer of the High Court,
Consultant on Probate and Administration
to the Incorporated Law Society of Ireland

PUBLISHED BY FORT PUBLICATIONS

First Edition: 1980
Reprinted: 1980
                   1981
                   1990
                   1993
                   1997
Second Edition: 1998
Third Edition: 2006

Fort Publications
10 D Carrickbrennan Road
Monkstown
Co. Dublin.
Telephone: 01 280 6248

ISBN 0-953-1880-2-7

Printed by Brunswick Press Limited,
Unit B2 Bluebell Ind. Est. Dublin 12.
Telephone: 456 9555
Fax: 456 9599

PREFACE

The idea for this book came from Prof. Laurence Sweeney, Director of Training for the Incorporated Law Society of Ireland, during the preparation of the first course for solicitors' apprentices under the new system of legal education. He felt that a brief summary of the basic features of Probate and Administration would not only be a most useful guideline for apprentices but would also prove a handy reference book for practitioners.

This book is aimed at achieving such an objective. It does not presume to be a definitive work on Probate law. It concentrates on fundamental practices and procedures and only touches peripherally on the vast area of the law, which is more fully expounded in text-books such as Millers's Irish Probate Practice, Tristam and Coote's Probate Practice, Mortimer's Probate Law and Practice, Jarman on Wills and Williams on Executors.

It is a cause for regret that Miller is out of print for many years and that no comprehensive work embracing Irish decisions, changes in statute law and changes in practice has been published since the State was established. In an effort to relieve this undesirable situation, I have been working on a larger book which I expect to have published in the not-too-distant future. In the meantime, I hope that this guideline will, at least, help to meet a current need.

I would like to express my thanks to Miss Stephanie Clear, a former Probate Officer, Prof. Richard Woulfe, Director of Education for the Incorporated Law Society of Ireland and Miss Anne Sweeney, solicitor, who read proofs and offered most helpful advice, although I take full responsibility for the contents. Lastly, I should like to thank the Incorporated Law Society of Ireland for its encouragement and support, and, in particular, for allowing me to use some precedent forms (Nos. 35 et seq.) from the work on The Succession Act, 1965 by William J. Maguire.

On a personal note, I should like to pay a special tribute to my wife for her assistance and patience in typing and proof-reading.

Eamonn G. Mongey, April 1980

CONTENTS

CHAPTER 1

PROBATE PRACTICE IN A NUTSHELL

Relevant Acts and Rules: The Succession Act 1965 (which came into operation on 1/1/1967)

The Administration of Estates Act 1959 (which applies to deaths between 1/6/1959 and 31/12/1966 incl.)

The Intestates Estates Act 1954 (which applies to deaths between 1/6/1954 and 31/12/1966 incl.)

The Rules of the Superior Courts - Orders 79 & 80 and Appendix Q.

(Note. References to sections of Acts in this book are to be taken as referring to the Succession Act, unless otherwise stated).

If a person dies having made a valid will he is said to have died *testate* and his assets are distributed, subject to some statutory limitations, and provided his assets are adequate, according to the terms of his will. If a person dies without having made a will he is said to have died *intestate* and his assets are distributed according to statute.

When a person dies, his assets are, as a general rule, frozen and no person can transfer any of his assets, giving a proper title or indemnifying himself, without a grant of representation. There are some exceptions to this e.g. joint property goes automatically to the survivor; small items, or small amounts of money, due by various firms or organisations may be delivered or paid without a grant.

ISSUE OF GRANTS

Grants of representation issue from the Probate Office, or from a District Probate Registry, both of which are part of the High Court. There are 14 District Probate Registries around Ireland, controlled by County Registrars, with authority to issue grants only where the deceased had a fixed place of abode in the counties within the jurisdiction of the particular District Registry. They are authorised to accept papers to lead to a grant by post. The Probate Office has all-Ireland jurisdiction, but is prohibited by Rule of Court (0.79 r.3) from accepting such papers by post.

PERSONAL REPRESENTATIVES

The term "personal representatives" includes, firstly, *executors,* i.e. persons nominated by a testator in his will to administer his estate and, secondly, *administrators,* i.e. persons appointed by the Court to undertake these duties where a person dies intestate, or where someone other than an executor is seeking to "prove" a will. The rules and methods by which such persons are chosen are referred to later.

Prior to the Administration of Estates Act 1959 only personal property devolved on the personal representative. Now, where a death occurs on or after the 1st June 1959, both real and personal property do. His functions are to collect all the assets of the deceased, pay all his debts and funeral expenses, and distribute the balance, either according to the terms of the particular will or according to statute.

KINDS OF GRANTS OF REPRESENTATION

1. **Grant of Probate** - given only to the executor, or executors, of a will.
2. **Grant of Administration with the Will Annexed** - given where there is a will but where somebody other than an executor applies for a grant.
3. **Grant of Administration Intestate** - given when a person dies without having made a will.

4. **Second or Subsequent Grants** - given when a grant which has already been given in the same estate ceases e.g. by reason of the death of the grantee.
5. **Limited Grants** - can be limited as regards duration (e.g. during minority), purpose (e.g. to substantiate proceedings) or subject matter (e .g. trustee property).
6. **Special Grants** c.g. Section 31 (l) or Section 27 (4).

GRANTS OF REPRESENTATION GENERALLY

Representation of the real estate and personal estate may be granted either separately or together. (Section 28).

A grant of representation in respect of the estate of a deceased person may be extracted notwithstanding that the deceased left no estate in this jurisdiction (Section 29).

No grant may issue within l4 days of the death of a person unless the Court or Probate Officer orders otherwise (0.79 r.33).

Affidavits. Affidavits must be sworn before a Judge, Commissioner for Oaths or an officer of the High Court, empowered to administer oaths (0.40 r.5). They are not sufficient if sworn before a Peace Commissioner.

No affidavit shall be sufficient if sworn before the solicitor acting for the party on whose behalf the affidavit is to be used, or before any agent or correspondent.

The person before whom affidavits are taken shall certify in the affidavit to his knowledge of the deponent (0.40 r.14). This is usually done by the clause "I know deponent" in the jurat of the oath.

The deponents in a joint affidavit are not bound to swear the affidavit before the same commissioner.

Affidavits more than six months old should be re-sworn.

All alterations made in an affidavit or oath must be initialled by the Commissioner administering the oath. (0.40 r.13).

Where an affidavit is being sworn abroad, it should be sworn before an Irish diplomatic or consular representative or where there is none such convenient, then before a notary public or, in a country in the British Commonwealth, before any judge, court, notary public or person authorised to administer oaths (0.40 r.7).

Forms for use in Probate and Administration matters are set out mainly in Appendix Q of the Rules of the Superior Courts. Most of these are also available from law stationers. Some are set out in the Appendix to this book.

Fees. Probate fees are laid down in the Supreme Court and High Court (Fees) Order, which can be obtained from the Government Publications Sales Office, Molesworth St., Dublin, 2.

Scope. The operation of a grant of representation extracted in this jurisdiction is limited to the assets of the deceased within the Republic. Grants may have to be extracted in other countries to deal with assets in these countries.

CHAPTER 2

WILLS

A Will is a declaration in writing of a man's wishes providing for the distribution of his property after his death.

A Codicil is a supplement to a will, which alters or adds to it. The law relating to its execution is exactly the same as for wills.

A will need not be in any special form but it must comply with the requirements of the Succession Act.

REQUIREMENTS FOR A VALID WILL (Sections 77 & 78)

1. The will must be in writing.
2. The testator must be over 18 years or be, or have been, married.
3. He must be of sound disposing mind.
4. He must sign his name, make his mark or acknowledge his signature in the presence of two witnesses, present together.
5. His signature or mark must be at the end of the will.
6. The two witnesses must sign their names in his presence.

RECOMMENDED FORMAT FOR A WILL

  (i) Name and address of the testator.
  (ii) Revocation of earlier wills and codicils.
  (iii) Appointment of Executors (preferably more than one, giving addresses and relationship, if any).
  (iv) Dispositive provisions.
  (v) Residuary clause.
  (vi) Date.
  (vii) Signature of the testator.

(viii) Attestation clause —- "Signed by the testator in the presence of us and then signed by us in the presence of the testator."

(ix) Signatures of the witnesses, with addresses and descriptions.

Witnesses: If a beneficiary, or his or her spouse, witnesses a will, the gift to such witness is void, but the attestation is good (Section 82). If a solicitor/executor incorporates a charging clause in a will he loses his right to profit costs if he witnesses the will. An executor is admissible as a witness. (Section 84). An acknowledgement of his signature by a witness is not sufficient. Presence means visual presence. There are no age limits for witnesses but, since they may be called on to give evidence they should be neither too young nor too old.

ALTERATIONS IN WILL

Any alterations to a will must be authenticated in one of the following ways:

1. By the signatures or initials of the testator and witnesses in the margin (Section 86) *(The recommended way).*
2. Executed as is required for the execution of a Will (Section 86).
3. By the signatures of the testator and witnesses to a memo referring to the alteration (Section 86).
4. By the initials of the witnesses, if the alterations are of small importance (0.79 r.11).
5. By a recital in the attestation clause (0.79 r.11).
6. By re-execution of the will with a new attestation clause referring to the alteration (0.79 r.l0).
7. By a Codicil which refers to the alteration (0.79 r.10).
   Otherwise, evidence on affidavit will be required when proving the will.

Obliterations and Erasures of importance always require an affidavit (0.79 r.12).

INSTRUCTIONS FOR A WILL

These should always be retained by the solicitor. As a precautionary measure, if there is the likelihood of delay in executing the final draft of the will, the instructions may be executed as a will. Original wills should be lodged in the office safe and a record entered in the office Wills Register. Where the testator takes the original will away with him, a copy should be retained in the office.

INCORPORATION OF DOCUMENTS

Where a will refers to some other document or unexecuted paper, such as a list of furniture or jewellery or a map, it is, sometimes, necessary to incorporate such document and admit it to proof as part of the will. It can be incorporated by order of the Probate Officer.

Three requirements:
  (1) The document must be in actual existence at the time of execution of the will;
  (2) It must be referred to in the will as being in existence;
  (3) It must be clearly identified.

APPOINTMENT OF EXECUTORS

More than one should be appointed. The appointment must be unambiguous and the persons appointed should be clearly identified by full name, address, description and relationship to deceased (if any). A person may also be deemed to have been appointed *"according to the tenor"*, that is where he has been given some essential duties of an executor e.g. to pay deceased's debts.

Executors *must* be: (l) over 18 years and (2) not suffering from a legal disability, or they will not be allowed to extract a grant of Probate.

They *may* be:	(a)	an identifiable individual
	(b)	a trust corporation within the meaning of Section 30 of the Succession Act
	(c)	an office-holder e.g. a parish priest or a bank-manager
	(d)	a firm of solicitors but, unless otherwise stated, this means the partners at the date of the will.
They *can* be	(1)	substituted e.g. "I appoint A as my executor but should he predecease me, then I appoint B as my executor,"
	(2)	limited - in time, or to part of the estate.

An executor's title is derived from the will. Probate is the evidence of his title and it relates back to the testator's death. He can, therefore, perform certain acts (e.g. paying debts) before obtaining probate.

Executor de son tort: A person who wrongfully carries out the functions of an executor or an administrator, without having been so appointed.

FOREIGN CASES

A testamentary disposition, not validly executed in accordance with Section 78 of the Succession Act, may still, under Section 102, be valid as regards form if it complies with the internal law -

(a) of the place where it was made, or
(b) of the nationality, or
(c) domicile possessed by the testator at the date of his will or of his death, or
(d) of the place where the testator had his habitual residence, or
(e) in the case of immovables, of the place where they are situate.

Evidence. The evidence required to satisfy the Probate Office that a will fulfils one of these conditions must be in form of (1) a sealed and certified copy of the grant from the appropriate Court in the country concerned, or (2) an affidavit of law from a lawyer practising, or who has practised, in that jurisdiction. Where a will is in a foreign language, an application may be made to the Probate Officer to prove it in terms of a translation (O.79 r.5(10)).

This application is made in advance of preparing the papers for the proposed grant. The Probate Officer will make the Order provided the following proofs are in order:

(a) that it was executed according to the law of the particular country;

(b) who is entitled to administer the estate;

(c) the competence of the translator.

In exceptional cases, e.g., where a person might seek to take a grant limited to a particular part of the estate, an application must be made to court. (O.79 r.21).

(Note. If the application is not being made by (or on behalf of) an executor, the affidavit should also show who is entitled to administer the estate according to the law of the domicile).

England, Wales & Northern Ireland. If the country concerned is England, Wales or Northern Ireland the will will normally be accepted as duly executed if it has been executed according to the Irish Succession Act.

Scotland. In Scotland the grant issued takes the form of a Confirmation and the original will is returned to the solicitor. The original will (or a sealed and certified copy) together with a sealed and certified copy of the Confirmation must be lodged when applying in Ireland.

Sometimes it may be desirable to make one will dealing with the property here and another dealing with property abroad. Care should be taken in drafting the later of these wills to avoid revoking the former.

Probate may be granted of two or more wills where they are not wholly inconsistent and where the later will contains no revocation clause. If, however, one is expressed to deal with property abroad, only the other will be proved here, although both wills must be produced to the Probate Officer for perusal.

A Joint Will is a single instrument executed by two, or more, persons and expressing the testamentary wishes of each. Its usefulness is limited. It can be revoked at any time, and by either party, as far as it applies to him.

Mutual Wills are two testamentary documents, executed by two persons, each giving substantially identical rights to the other. Most of them are simple husband-and-wife situations. They are revocable, but they may amount to a compact in equity, if, for example, they were made pursuant to a special agreement.

In each of the above two cases the will can be proved on the death of either testator.

REVOCATION OF A WILL

A feature of a will is that it cannot be made so as to be irrevocable. It may be revoked in any of the following ways, under Section 85:

(1) By subsequent marriage, unless made in contemplation of *that* marriage.

(2) By another will or codicil.

(3) By a writing executed as required for a will.

(4) By burning, tearing or destruction by the testator, or by someone, in his presence, and by his direction with intention to revoke.

Dependent Relative Revocation. This awkward phrase simply means that where it can be established that the revocation of a will was conditional on the happening of an event which did not occur, or upon some belief which turned out to be wrong, there is no revocation.

Revival. Where a will has been revoked, it can be revived only (1) by re-executing it or (2) by executing a codicil showing an intention to revive it.

WILL SPEAKS FROM DEATH

A will speaks from the death of the testator (Section 89), unless a contrary intention appears in the will; for example, the provisions of the relevant statutes apply only to deaths which occurred, or occur, after they came into operation (with some exceptions); office-holders appointed as executors must be those who held office at the date of death; distribution of a deceased's estate depends entirely on the circumstances existing at the date of death, thereby conclusively fixing the beneficiaries.

PROOF OF WILL

Solemn Form. A will is proved in solemn form when it is declared valid following a Court Action, in which evidence is given.

Common Form. A will is proved in common form when it is admitted to proof in the Probate Office or District Probate Registry, without any litigation.

CHAPTER 3

GRANTS OF PROBATE

An executor has the first right to prove a will. The type of grant issued to him is called a Probate. If he does not wish to "prove", he may renounce his rights. On the other hand, any one of two or more executors may apply for a grant of probate without notice to the other executor(s), and simply reserve the rights of those other executor(s).

The documents *necessary* to extract a Grant of Probate are as follows:

(1) Notice of application.
(2) Original Will and Codicil (if any)
(3) Engrossment of same.
(4) Oath of Executor.
(5) Inland Revenue Affidavit with Form C.A. (for lands and buildings).
(6) Death Certificate.
     Documents which *may be required* in certain cases:
(7) Affidavit of due execution of Will or Codicil.
(8) Affidavit of plight and condition.
(9) Affidavit of testamentary capacity.
(10) Renunciation of Executor.
(11) Resolution of Trust Corporation.
(12) Miscellaneous Affidavits e.g. identity of executor or of deceased.

(1) **Notice of Application**
This may be lodged without the other papers and has the effect of a Caveat in preventing any other grant issuing in the estate.

(2) **Original Will and Codicil (if any)**
The will, codicil and any other testamentary document must be exhibited in the Oath i.e. initialled or signed by both the

18

executor(s) and Commissioner for Oaths *on the back* or elsewhere so as to be clearly distinguishable from the will itself and its attestation (0.79 r.38).

(3)   Engrossment of Will and Codicil (if any)
This is the copy of the will which will be subsequently included in the original Grant of Probate. It may be in manuscript, typed, printed or in the form of a photocopy provided it is a clear, legible copy on durable paper. It should also have a backing sheet. The paper should be A4 size, (297mm x 210 mm) and there should be a margin of approximately 35mms on the left-hand side.

Alterations. The engrossment should be a plain copy of the original, no corrections being made in the spelling. It should be written without a break. Where interlineations are admitted to proof, they should not be so interlined, but inserted in their proper place - similarly with other alterations.

Certificate. At the foot of every engrossment, leaving a space of approximately 25mms below the last words of the will, there should be a certificate signed by the solicitor that it is a true copy of the original will (and codicil, if any), or of a sealed and certified copy (if the will has already been proved in another country).

(4)   Oath of Executor (Form No. 3 Appendix Q.)
Name and Address. The name, address and description of the deceased and of the executor must be given. If a different name is used both names should be given e.g. John otherwise Jack. If a different address appears in the will, the other address should also be given with the words "formerly of" or "in will erroneously stated to be of", as the case may be. Sometimes it is required to have former addresses of deceased set out in the grant where stocks and shares are registered in the name of the deceased at a former address. If there are more than three addresses, an order of the Probate Officer is necessary.

Description. Description means occupation as far as males are concerned. Females may give either their occupation or their marital status (spinster, widow or married woman). Where deceased's widow who has re-married is applying, she should be described as "relict of deceased".

A person with no particular occupation can be described as "Gentleman". If he is retired he may be described as "Retired ...." or "Pensioner".

Where the original will is not being proved the oath should be amended to read "A sealed and certified copy of the true and original last will" or, as the case may be.

Relationship. The relationship of the executor to the deceased should be given. If he is not a blood relation, he should be described as a stranger-in-blood.

Several Executors. Where several executors are appointed by will, all may apply, or one or more only, the others renouncing their rights, or having them reserved. The proving executor(s) need not notify any other executor. It is sufficient to state in the oath "reserving the rights of the other executor". An executor whose rights are reserved may apply for a Grant of Double Probate while the acting executor is alive.

Where one or more executors have died the proving executor should describe himself as "the surviving executor" or "one of the surviving executors".

Where an executor has renounced, the renunciation must be exhibited in the oath.

Office-holder. Where the holder of a particular office is appointed as executor he must swear that he was the office-holder "for the time being at the date of death and, as such, the executor named in said will".

Firm of Solicitors. Where a firm of solicitors is appointed it is the members of the firm *at the date of the will* who may act, and they must swear accordingly - unless the will provides otherwise.

Substituted. An executor may also be substituted. The reason for the substitution e.g. the death of the first-named executor, or the happening of some other contingency or fulfilment of a condition, must be stated in the oath.

Trust Corporation. If a trust corporation is named as an executor the resolution nominating a person to swear all the documents necessary to apply for a Grant of Probate on its behalf must be exhibited and the way in which the trust corporation qualifies as such under Section 30 of the Succession Act must be clearly stated.

Trust corporations under Section 30 fall into three categories:

(1) a corporation appointed by the High Court in any particular case to be a trustee;

(2) a corporation empowered by its constitution to undertake trust business, and having a place of business in the State or in Northern Ireland, and being (a) an Associated Bank under the Central Bank Act 1942 or (b) a company which fulfils certain conditions;

(3) a corporation which satisfies the President of the High Court that it undertakes the administration of any charitable, ecclesiastical or public trust without remuneration, e.g. The Representative Church Body, The Maynooth Mission to China, The Irish Cancer Society.

Banks and companies which are entitled to extract grants in other countries, but which do not qualify as trust corporations here, must appoint attorneys to extract grants (of administration) in this jurisdiction.

Assets. The gross estate (real and personal) of the deceased within this jurisdiction as appearing in the Certificate for the High Court attached to the Inland Revenue Affidavit should be inserted in the oath.

(5)   Inland Revenue Affidavit

The original affidavit, with one copy, should be sent to the Revenue Commissioners, Dublin Castle. The copy will be returned with a certificate for the High Court concerning the payment of estate duty (for deaths prior to 1st April 1975) or inheritance tax (for deaths on or after that date) and this copy must be lodged with the other Probate papers. No inventories or valuations need be attached to the copy affidavit.

Form C.A.6. If the estate includes land and/or buildings *three* copies of a form C.A.6. (or D.1) should be completed and forwarded to the Revenue Commissioners. One will be returned and this should also be lodged with the other Probate papers.

(6)   **Affidavit of due execution of will or codicil**

When required:

1. Where there is no attestation clause;
2. Where the attestation clause is defective (for example, by not setting out clearly that the will was executed according to statute);
3. Where the testator's signature appears in the attestation clause;
4. Where the testator's signature appears below those of the witnesses;
5. Where the testator signs twice.
    In all the above cases, however, if there is a codicil which clearly identifies the will and which contains a good attestation clause, the affidavit is dispensed with.
6. Where the testator signs by mark;
7. Where the testator's signature is feeble or indecipherable;
8. Where the testator's signature is made on his behalf by another person;
9. Where the testator is blind.
    In Nos. 6 to 9 inclusive, the affidavit must contain an averment that the will was read over to the testator and that he appeared to understand it, even if the attestation clause contains such a statement.
    If the testator was blind there must be a further averment that the witnesses signed their names in such a position that he could have seen them so sign if he had his eyesight.
10. Where the will is undated, or contains different dates, or if any doubt arises about the date of due execution.
11. Where the will is written on several sheets of paper; (Here the affidavit must show that all the sheets were in the same room at the time of execution).
12. Where there are any interlineations, alterations, (unless duly authenticated) erasures or obliterations (which always require an affidavit, where they are of importance). All amendments must be specifically referred to in the affidavit. It is not sufficient to say "all the amendments etc."

If no evidence is forthcoming concerning amendments to wills they are presumed to have been made after execution.

Note. If there is a likelihood that an affidavit, concerning the execution of a will, will be called for it is advisable to swear one at the time of making the will.

Who may make such affidavits?

(a) Attesting witnesses. When making any affidavit to admit a will to proof, such witness must deal with due execution (0.79 r.41). If evidence cannot be obtained from the attesting witnesses, then -

(b) Persons present at the execution who were not witnesses

(c) Persons who drafted the will, or read it over to the testator - as far as amendments are concerned

(d) Otherwise, an application must be made to Court, giving evidence of the handwriting of the deceased and of the witnesses and of any circumstances which may raise a presumption in favour of due execution (0.79 r.9).

Note. For precedents, see Appendix (No. 2).

Will Condemned

The Probate Officer will refuse probate of a will if satisfied, after perusing the affidavits of both attesting witnesses, that the requirements of the statute were not complied with (0.79 r.7). He may also refuse probate of part of a will.

(7)   **Affidavit of plight and condition of will or codicil**

When required:

(a) If the will has any pin-holes, clip-marks or traces of adhesive;

(b) If the will has a torn edge or top or bottom.
    For (a) or (b) evidence will be required showing how they occurred and stating that nothing of a testamentary nature was attached to the will or codicil.

(c) If there are any tears, burns, obliterations or attempted cancellations. Evidence will be required to show that the testator did not intend to revoke the will or codicil.

Who may make such affidavits.

(i)   Attesting witnesses;

(ii) The person responsible for the mark, tear, etc.;

(iii) The person in whose custody the will was retained;

(iv) The person who found the will.
Note. For precedents, see Appendix (No. 2).

(8)   **Affidavit of testamentary capacity**
When required:
(a)   Where a testator dies in a mental institution;
(b)   Where the will was made while the testator was in a mental institution;
(c)   Where any doubt arises about a testator's mental capacity.
Who may make such affidavits
(i)   The doctor who was attending the testator at the time he made the will; if medical evidence is not forthcoming, then -
(ii) The solicitor who drew the will; otherwise -
(iii) Any other responsible person who can give conclusive evidence about the testator's mental capacity.
Note. See Appendix (Nos. 23 & 24).

(9)   **Renunciation of Executor**
It must be in writing signed by the renunciant in the presence of any disinterested witness. It must be marked as an exhibit by the applicant for the grant and by the commissioner. The renunciant must state that he is over 18 years.

An executor who has intermeddled in the estate of a deceased may not renounce without the permission of the Court. A renunciant may retract his renunciation up to the issue of the Grant. He cannot renounce after he has extracted a grant.

An executor who renounces cannot take a grant in any other capacity without an order of the Court.

Where an executor has renounced probate of a will proved in another country, he must also renounce in this country before a grant will be given to a person with an inferior title. See Appendix (No. l0).

Infant or P.U.M. Neither an infant nor a person of unsound mind can renounce his right to executorship. The usual practice is to give a grant of administration with will annexed to the guardian or committee, respectively. A committee may, however, renounce on behalf of a person of unsound mind.

(10) Resolution of Trust Corporation

A trust corporation must apply for a grant through an officer nominated for that purpose. The nomination is made by resolution of the governing body or board of directors. A copy of the resolution, under the seal of the corporation, must be exhibited in the Oath, which is sworn by the nominee.

(11) Special affidavits

For example affidavit of identity of the executor or of the deceased or affidavit of law. See Appendix (No. 25).

CHAPTER 4

GRANT OF LETTERS OF ADMINISTRATION WITH WILL ANNEXED

A grant of administration with the will annexed is the grant issued where a will is proved by someone other than an executor.

When it arises:

(1) Where a testator has omitted to name an Executor;
(2) Where the Executor or Executors have died without proving the will;
(3) Where they have renounced, or have been deemed to have renounced, having failed to appear to a citation;
(4) Where the appointment of the Executor is void (by reason of uncertainty);
(5) Where the Executor is under a disability e.g. infant, person of unsound mind, or body not a trust corporation;
(6) Where the Executor is living abroad or suffers from a severe continuing physical disability and appoints an attorney;
(7) Where the Grant is made pursuant to Section 27(4), and there is a will involved.

Who is entitled:

The order of entitlement may appear complicated, but, in most cases, it depends on who is entitled to the residue, and the residuary legatee or the residuary devisee, simpliciter, is the most usual applicant.

The order of entitlement for deaths on, or since, 1/6/1959 is as follows:

(a) Universal or Residuary legatees or devisees in trust (if any). Their personal representative can never take a grant.
(b) Universal or Residuary legatees or devisees who are entitled beneficially (if any).
(c) Residuary legatees or devisees for life (if any). Their personal representative can never take a grant. See 0.79 r.5 (6)(d).

(d) Residuary legatees or devisees in remainder (if any). See 0.79 r.5 (6)(d).

(e) Persons entitled on intestacy (where the residue has lapsed or has not been disposed of).

(f) Legal personal representatives of beneficial Residuary legatees or devisees (who have survived the deceased) or of persons entitled on Intestacy. See also 0.79 r.5 (9)(b).

(g) Legatees and devisees - only entitled on the renunciation of those entitled to the residue. (See (b), (d), (e) and (f) above.)

(h) Creditors - pursuant to Court order or Probate Officer's 0.79 r.5 (6)(g).

(i) State - through the Attorney-General or Chief State Solicitor - where a person dies intestate as to all or part of his estate without any known relation and without any other person having an interest in the estate (Section 72 and 0.79 rr.64 & 65).

Clearing off clause:

The Oath of Admon. W.A. must be so worded as to clear off all persons having a prior right to the grant (0.79 r.28). There is no necessity to clear off trust interests, life interests or remainder interests unless such are expressly mentioned in the will.

The grant may be made without clearing off the residuary devisee or heir-at-law where the oath says that there is no real estate or that the deceased was not possessed of any real estate other than freehold land registered under Part IV of the Registration of Title Act 1891.

Note: For precedents see Appendix: (No. 20).

Death prior to 1st June 1959:

Devisees (including residuary, universal, beneficial or in trust) need not be cleared off in making title where the death occurred prior to 1/6/1959.

Residue

To constitute a gift of the residue there must be a disposition of the whole of the residue of the estate. In no case will a specific gift of property, even though it comprises all the known estate of the deceased be considered a gift of residue. In such cases the law always presumes a residue and a grant of Admon. W.A. will be given to those entitled on intestacy. See also 0.79 r.5 (6)(e) for Probate Officer's discretion.

Residuary Devisee is the person to whom the residue of the real estate has been left. A gift of "the rest of my land" also constitutes the beneficiary as residuary devisee.

Residuary Legatee is the person to whom the residue of the personal estate is left. Certain ambiguous phrases and words have been held to constitute the beneficiary as residuary legatee, where the context does not restrict the meaning e.g. "effects", "all my insurances and personal effects", "all my home and personal belongings", and "all moneys of which I die possessed".

Joint Residuary Legatees or Devisees. All must apply for a grant. If only one applies, the others must consent. Only the personal representative of the survivor is entitled to a grant. If they take as tenants in common, any one of them may apply without reference to the others. On the death of them all, the personal representative of any of them may apply.

Lapse

If a legatee or devisee dies in the lifetime of the testator, the legacy or devise lapses and, as a rule, if otherwise undisposed of, falls into the residue.

Where a share in the residue lapses it goes as on an intestacy, unless otherwise provided for in the will. However, where two legatees or devisees are joint tenants, and one dies before the testator, the lapsed share goes to the other.

Where there has been a partial failure of the residuary disposition, the persons entitled on an intestacy are equally entitled to extract a grant with the residuary legatees or devisees whose shares have not lapsed.

Spes Successionis: Administration W.A. under "spes

successionis" may be granted to the child of a universal legatee and devisee on his renunciation and consent. This does not apply to a residuary legatee and devisee. If he renounces, a legatee or devisee takes the grant. 0.79 r.5 (12) + (13).

Documents necessary to obtain a Grant of Letters of Administration with Will annexed

(1)   Notice of Application
(2)   Original Will (and Codicil, if any)
(3)   Engrossment of same
(4)   Oath for Admon. W/A
(5)   Inland Revenue Affidavit and Form C.A.6 (for land and buildings)
(6)   Bond (3 different forms)
(7)   Death Certificate

Documents which *may be required* in certain cases:

(8)   Justification of sureties
(9)   Affidavit of market value (for real estate)
(10)   Affidavit of Due Execution of Will or Codicil
(11)   Affidavit of plight and condition
(12)   Affidavit of testamentary capacity
(13)   Renunciation (See Appendix (No. 10))
(14)   Resolution of Trust Corporation
(15)   Miscellaneous affidavits.

The majority of these forms are the same as those used for extracting a grant of probate. The following are the exceptions:

(4)   **Oath of Admon. W.A.**

It must clear off all prior interests (e.g. executor) and clearly show how the applicant is entitled to the grant. The assets must be shown separately-the personal estate as contained in the Inland Revenue Affidavit and real estate according to the affidavit of market value. Specimen titles are set out in the Appendix (No. 20).

(6)   **Bond**

Always required. There are three different kinds depending on the date of death. That for deaths on or since 1st January 1967 is headed "Administration Bond" and should have the penultimate clause deleted. (The same form is also used in intestacy cases, when the penultimate clause is not deleted). The other two forms are headed Administration with Will Annexed Bond, one applying to deaths prior to 1/6/1959 (dealing only with personal estate) and the intermediate bond (1/6/1959 to 31/12/1966 incl.) dealing with all the estate. (See forms in Appendix).

Penal Sum. The penal sum must be for at least, double the gross assets (real and personal), as shown in the Oath.

Title. The title of the applicant (e.g. "the residuary legatee of" or "the lawful son of") must be shown.

Execution. It must be executed before the same Commissioner who administers the Oath, unless the Court or Probate Officer orders otherwise. It cannot be attested by the solicitor or agent of the party who executes it.

By practice direction of the President of the High Court (1st September, 2004), a person applying for administration shall not be required to furnish a surety of sureties in addition to the administration bond unless required to do so by the High Court, the Probate Officer or, in the case of a grant from a District Probate Registry, the District Probate Registrar. If such surety or sureties are Required, personal sureties, insurance companies or guarantee societies may so act.

Assignment of Bond. Where it appears to the High Court that the condition of an administration bond has been broken, the High Court may order that the bond be assigned to any person and such person may sue thereon in his own name.

(7)   Justification of Surety

Every surety must swear he is worth at least half the penal sum in the bond. He should be resident within the jurisdiction. He may be related to the applicant and may even be entitled to a share in the estate. No practising solicitor, clerk or apprentice may act as surety without leave of the Court or the Probate Officer.

(8)   **Affidavit of Market Value**

Required where the estate includes real estate, though an exception is generally made where Labourer's Act cottages or ground rents are involved. It may be made only by an auctioneer, valuer, farmer or Chartered Surveyor. It must be a current value. See Appendix (No. 8). Any milk quota should be included. A practitioner may certify by letter the value of non-agricultural real property or any leasehold property.

CHAPTER 5

GRANT OF LETTERS OF ADMINISTRATION INTESTATE

Grant Follows Interest

Where a person dies without having made a valid will he is, as we have seen in Chapter 1, said to have died intestate and his estate is distributed according to statute. An important consequence of the right to take a share in the estate of a deceased is that it also confers on the person entitled a right to extract a grant of administration intestate. The two are inseparable on the principle that the grant follows the interest. It must be emphasised that this interest is decided at the date of death when those entitled are conclusively fixed.

The interest of persons in the estate of an intestate has been varied by the Succession Act (which applies to deaths on, or after 1/1/1967). The changes are set out in detail in the Appendix (No. 14) and they apply to all the estate, both real and personal. This established the order in which persons became entitled to extract a grant of administration as set out hereunder and also in chart form in the Appendix (No. 15).

Non-marital blood relations are entitled under the Status of Children Act, 1987, where the deceased died on, or after, the 14/6/1988; and adopted children since the Adoption Act, 1952.

Order of entitlement to extract a grant for deaths on or since 1/1/1967

(1) Surviving spouse (See also 0.79 r.5(1)(b).
(2) Next of kin, as follows:
　　(a) Child or other descendant (See also parties entitled in distribution)
　　(b) Father or mother, equally entitled
　　(c) Brother or sister (See also parties entitled in distribution)

(d) Nephew or niece
(e) Grandparent
(f) Uncle or aunt
(g) Great grandparent
(h) First cousin (cousin german), great-uncle or great-aunt, grand-nephew or grand-niece
(i) Great great grandparent
(j) Other next-of-kin depending on degrees of blood relationship, with any direct lineal ancestors being postponed to other relatives in the same degree.

(3) Parties entitled in distribution.

(4) Personal representatives of spouse, next-of-kin or persons entitled in distribution. 0.79 r.5(2) + (9)(b).

(5) Persons entitled under "Spes Successionis". 0.79 r.5(12).

(6) Creditors–pursuant to Court Order or Probate Officer's – 0.79 r.5(4).

(7) The State, as the ultimate intestate successor-where there are no known next-of-kin or any other person with an interest in the estate (Section 73 and 0.79 rr. 65 & 66).

Note. Any member of a class entitled to share in the estate may apply for a grant without reference to the others. Primogeniture gives no priority.

(2) **Next-of-kin**. While the guiding principle in establishing the next-of-kin is based on the degrees of blood relationship, there have been departures from this, as can be seen from the right to entitlement e.g. giving preference to all descendants, however remote, over ancestors and collaterals. In deciding on entitlement, relations of the *half-blood* are entitled with the whole blood. Step-relations have no entitlement.

(3) **Parties entitled in distribution.** Where a widow or widower dies intestate, leaving a child or children, any grandchildren or other descendants who are the issue of a predeceased child take the share of their parent between them. This taking by representation is known as taking "per stirpes". On the death or renunciation of the surviving child or children, those taking per stirpes may apply for a grant.

The same principle applies where brothers and sisters are entitled and where there are nephews or nieces who are the issue of a predeceased brother or sister.

This doctrine of taking "per stirpes" is not allowed in any other instances except as above.

(4) Personal representatives of spouse, next-of-kin or of persons entitled in distribution. If the spouse, next-of-kin and parties entitled in distribution are either dead or have renounced, administration will be granted to the personal representative of anyone of them.

Where the personal representatives are co-executors the practice is to allow any one of them to apply for a grant, but where they are co-administrators they must apply jointly or those who do not wish to act must renounce.

(5) Spes Successionis. Administration may be granted to the child of person who is entitled to all the estate on the renunciation and consent of such person, on the basis that such child has a hope of succeeding to his parent's estate. Exceptionally, administration may be granted to the child of one of a number of persons entitled where they all renounce and consent.

(6) Creditors.

(7) The State. Where there are no known next-of-kin of an intestate the State takes the estate as the ultimate intestate successor (Section 73(1)). In such a case, the Attorney General usually nominates the Chief State Solicitor to take the grant on his behalf, though he has power to nominate anyone.

Under Section 73 (2), however, the Minister for Finance may waive the right of the State in favour of a particular person. The only way in which such a person can extract a grant is under Section 27 (4).

Deaths prior to the Succession Act
While the Succession Act varied the rules as to succession on intestacy, and thereby the right to extract a grant of

Administration, the right to extract had already been varied prior to that by the Administration of Estates Act 1959, which applies to deaths between 1/6/1959 and 31/12/1966 inclusive.

The 1959 Act changed title in two respects -

(a)   It gave a widow a priority for all time to apply for a grant to her deceased husband. (Up to that she had priority for only three months).

(b)   It vested both *real* and *personal* estate in the personal representatives. (Up to that only personal estate and freehold registered land vested in him). The result was that the heir-at-law became equally entitled with the next-of-kin to a grant, but under a different set of rules, which are set out below.

Order of entitlement to extract a grant for deaths prior to 1/1/1967 (excluding the heir-at-law)

(1)   Surviving spouse

(2)   Next-of-kin (in different order):

(a)   Child or other descendant (or the issue of a predeceased child)

(b)   Father

(c)   Mother

(d)   Brother or sister (or the child of a predeceased brother or sister)

(e)   Grandparent

(f)   Uncle or aunt, nephew or niece or great grandparent

(g)   First cousin, great-uncle or great-aunt, grand-nephew or grand-niece, great great grandparent

(h)   Other next-of-kin depending on degrees of blood relationship.

Changes in entitlement of surviving spouse

Husband: Where a married woman died prior to 1/6/1959 the surviving husband took all the personal estate and so was the only person entitled to a grant. If he renounced, no one was entitled. If he died only his personal representative was.

35

For a death between 1/6/1959 and 31/12/1966 inclusive, the husband also had a priority to the grant, but if he died or renounced, her heir-at-law was the next person entitled.

For a death on or since 1/1/1967 the husband still has a priority. If he dies or renounces her issue are next entitled, as they now take one-third share in the estate. If she has no issue, and if he renounces, no one is entitled. On his death his personal representative, only, is entitled.

Widow: Where a married man died prior to 1/6/1959 the widow had a priority, but only for 3 months. After that, or if she died or renounced, the next of kin were equally entitled. They took two-thirds of the personal estate if they were issue; half if they were not.

For deaths since 1/6/1959, the widow has a priority for all time. If her husband died between 1/6/1959, and 31/12/1966 inclusive and she renounces or dies the next-of-kin and heir-at-law are entitled equally.

For a death on, or since, 1/1/1967 a widow takes all the estate if her husband dies intestate *without issue,* so she is the only person entitled to a grant in these circumstances. If she renounces nobody is entitled to a grant. If she subsequently dies, only her personal representative is. If there are issue, they are entitled next after the widow.

Note. A common-law wife, cannot succeed to the estate of her common-law husband, should he die intestate.

Where a married couple have been legally separated or are living apart, and one of them dies intestate, the survivor must renounce his, or her, rights before any of the next-of-kin will be given a grant. Failing such renunciation, an application must be made to Court for an order under Section 27 (4). Where a person who has been divorced in Ireland dies intestate, his next-of-kin can apply for a grant without reference to the other divorced spouse.

Rules for tracing the heir-at-law:

(1)   Descent was traced from the last purchaser i.e. the person who acquired the land other than on intestacy or by escheat, partition or enclosure;

(2)   The issue (children, grandchildren, etc.) were preferred to other relatives, males being preferred to females;

(3)   Where there were two or more males of equal degree, the eldest only inherited (primogeniture), but females all shared equally as coparceners;

(4)   The issue of a deceased person represented him ad infinitum;

(5)   On failure of issue, the nearest lineal ancestor succeeded to the inheritance;

(6)   Paternal ancestors were preferred to maternal ancestors;

(7)   The mother of a more remote male paternal ancestor and her heirs were preferred to the mother of a less remote male paternal ancestor and her heirs;

(8)   On failure of paternal ancestors and their issue, similar rules applied to the maternal ancestors and their issue;

(9)   Where the common ancestor was a male, relatives of the half-blood inherited next after relatives of the whole blood of the same degree, but where the common ancestor was a female they inherited next after her.

Documents which are necessary when applying for a grant of Administration Intestate:

(i)   **Notice of application.**

(ii)   **Oath of Administrator.** It must be so worded as to clear off all persons having a prior right to a grant. As making title can present difficulties, specimen titles are set out in the Appendix(Nos. 16,17, 18& 19).

(iii)   **Bond.** There are three different forms, depending on date of death. (See notes on Admon. W.A. Bond). The two forms in use for deaths prior to 1/1/1967 are headed "Administration Intestate Bond." (See forms in Appendix).

(iv)   **Inland Revenue Affidavit and Form C.A.6** (for land and buildings).

(v)   **Death Certificate.**

Documents which may be required:

(vi)   Justification of sureties (only where there is a personal surety).

(vii)   Affidavit of Market Value.

(viii) Renunciation (See Appendix (No. 9)).
(ix) Resolution of Trust Corporation.
(x) Miscellaneous affidavits (e.g. heirship or of law).

The same rules apply to above documents as for Probate and Admon. W.A. cases.

Joint Grant. More than one person in the same class, or in the same degree of entitlement, may apply for a joint grant, which expires only on the death of the surviving grantee. Not more than 3 may apply unless Probate Officer otherwise directs. 0.79 r.5(14).

Sources of Information when Tracing Next-of-kin.

(1) Local Registrar (2) General Register Office, Joyce House, 8 Lombard St., E Dublin 2 (3) Family (4) Advertisement (5) Church Records (6) Headstones (7) Census of Population (8) National Archives, Bishop St., Dublin 8 (9) Local Newspapers.

Domicile. When an intestate dies domiciled outside the Republic of Ireland but leaving property in the Republic, the grant will be given according to the law of the domicile where the property is movable, but according to the Irish law (Lex Situs) where the property is immovable.

The evidence to establish entitlement according to the law of the domicile must be in the form of (l) a sealed and certified copy of the grant from the Court of the domicile or, if there is no such grant, then (2) an affidavit of law from an advocate practising, or who has practised in the country of domicile. Affidavits of the law of Great Britain, Northern Ireland, the Channel Islands and the Isle of Man may be taken from a solicitor.

CHAPTER 6

LIMITED GRANTS AND SPECIAL GRANTS

Grants may be limited in any way the Court thinks fit (Sect 26(1). They may be limited as regards -
(A) Duration; (B) Purpose; (C) Subject-matter.

(A) GRANTS LIMITED AS TO DURATION
The following are the most common of such grants:
(1) **Grant to guardian of infant** (under 18 years)
     Guardians may be -
     (a) Testamentary i.e. appointed by a parent by Will (A Petition, as described below, is required, but an Election by the infants is not).
     (b) Appointed by the President of the High Court in his Wards of Court jurisdiction (Petition required only where the President's Order omits to authorise application for a grant. No Election required).
     (c) Appointed by the Probate Officer pursuant to 0.79 rr. 24 & 25. (Petition always required. Election required unless petitioner is the parent of the infant)
     (d) Appointed by the Circuit Court or District Court under the Guardianship of Infants Act, 1964, as amended by the Courts Act, 1981. (Petition always required. No Election required).

Procedure. Where a Petition is being used in any of the above, it is lodged (with Election, where necessary) with the Probate Officer who will, if satisfied, make an order giving liberty to proposed guardian to extract a grant, limited for the use and benefit of the infant(s) and during their incapacity. The Petition, Election and Order are lodged with the other papers when applying for a grant of administration. The Order must be referred to in the Oath. An Election, when required as set out above, should contain the expressed wishes of any infant over 12 years. The Guardian so elected takes the grant for the benefit of all the infants.

Contents of Petition: The Petition must show -
  (i) that the petitioner is next-of-kin of the infants or that nearer kin have renounced;
  (ii) that there is no other guardian, testamentary or otherwise;
  (iii) that the petitioner has no interest antagonistic to that of the infants;
  (iv) with whom they are residing;
  (v) the value of the estate;
  (vi) the ages of the children.
  See Appendix (No. 31).

Election: See Appendix (No. 30).

Priority: A person of full age, equally interested with an infant, is entitled in priority to the guardian of such infant. (0.79 r.5 (1) (l)).

(2) **Grant to Committee of person of unsound mind**
  (a) If he is a Ward of Court, the President of the High Court generally makes an order giving liberty to the committee to apply for a grant
  (b) If he is not a Ward of Court, the Probate Officer may make an order appointing a committee to extract a grant. It is made on foot of an affidavit from the proposed committee, setting out all the facts, and a further affidavit from a doctor, giving conclusive evidence that the person entitled to a grant is incapable of managing his affairs. A letter of consent should also be obtained from the Registrar of the Wards of Court.

Who is appointed Committee by Probate Officer?
In case of an executor's incapacity, it is the Residuary

40

Legatee or Devisee. In case of a person entitled to administration, it is his next-of-kin.

(c) Otherwise, an application must be made to Court.

Priority. A person equally entitled with a person of unsound mind is entitled in priority to the committee of such person (0.79. r.5 (1) (m).) Probate Officer may alter -0.79 r.5 (9)(c).

Procedure. The appropriate order must be lodged with all the usual papers to extract a Grant of Administration, which will be limited for the use and benefit of the person of unsound mind and during his incapacity.

(3)   **Grant to Attorney**
If the person entitled to a grant is residing out of, or about to leave, the jurisdiction or is suffering from a severe, continuing physical disability, administration, or administration with the will annexed, may be granted to his attorney (O.79 r.23). The grant is limited for the use and benefit of the donor and until he himself shall apply for and obtain a grant. See Appendix (Nos. 12 & 13).

Execution: The power of attorney may be executed before any disinterested witness but it is desirable to have it executed before a notary public or person empowered to administer oaths.

Persons entitled within jurisdiction. A grant will not be given to the attorney of an executor who is outside the jurisdiction, if there are any executors residing within the jurisdiction. These latter must first renounce. This does not apply to persons within the jurisdiction who are entitled to administration.

Procedure: The power of attorney must be exhibited in the Oath for Administrator which must also show the address and description of the donor and say that he is

41

over 18 years. The other documents are the same as those required for a grant of administration.

Note. If the power of attorney is a general one, it should first be enrolled, or filed, in the Central Office. An enduring power of attorney cannot be used to establish title to a grant on behalf of the donor. (Section 16, Power of Attorney Act, 1996).

(4)   **Grant Pendente lite**
Where any legal proceedings are pending, touching the validity of the will of a deceased person or for obtaining, recalling or revoking any grant, the High Court may grant administration to whomsoever it wishes.

Limitations: (1) The administrator may not distribute the estate;
(2) He is subject to the immediate control of the court and acts under its direction;
(3) The grant expires on the termination of the suit, including any appeal.

Procedure: (a) Application for an order under Section 27(7) may be made in the proceedings (on the contentious side of the Court) or to the Probate Judge
(b) When applying for a grant all the usual papers, including a bond, must be filed together with a copy of the Court order
(c) When the proceedings are terminated, application is made for a general grant.

(5)   **Grant where original will is lost**
This calls for an application to the Court which, if satisfied, will make order to prove the will in terms of a copy. The grant will be limited until the original, or a more authentic copy thereof, be lodged in the Probate Office.

(B)   GRANTS LIMITED FOR A PURPOSE
The following are the most common of such grants:

(1)   **Grant to substantiate proceedings**

Where a person wishes to take proceedings against a deceased's estate to which representation has not been raised by those entitled (e.g. where a driver of a car is killed in an accident in which the prospective plaintiff was injured), the Court may appoint an administrator, limited for the purpose of the proceedings.

Procedure: Application to Court under Section 27(4), with service of notice on those persons entitled to a general grant. It is also desirable to have issued a citation against those persons in the first instance. All the usual papers must be filed, including an Inland Revenue Affidavit (showing nominal assets), Bond and Court Order, when application is being made for a grant.

(2)   **Grant ad colligenda bona**

For the purpose of collecting and preserving, but not distributing the estate of the deceased.

Procedure: Application for an order (under Section 27 (4) unless the applicant is also entitled to a general grant) may be made in the proceedings (if they have issued) or to the Probate Judge. All the usual papers must be filed, together with a copy of the Court Order, when application is being made for a grant.

(3)   **Grant for a specific purpose** e.g. to complete a sale where the vendor has died.

Procedure: As for No. (1) above.

(C)   GRANTS LIMITED TO A PARTICULAR PART OF THE ESTATE
The following are the most common of such grants:

(1)   **Trustee Grant**. Where the deceased is the sole surviving trustee of any property and where he has no other

property of his own, a grant will be issued to the person entitled to a general grant but limited to the trust property. If the person so entitled is not the proposed applicant a Court order is necessary.

Procedure: All the usual papers including a special Inland Revenue Affidavit (Form A 4) must be filed. The Oath must be amended to show that deceased was possessed only of trust property. Special (low) Probate fees are charged.

(2) **Limited Wills and Limited Executors**
A person may make a number of wills, one to deal with his estate within this jurisdiction and one to deal with his estate abroad. Only the will specifically limited to property within this jurisdiction will be admitted to proof and the grant will be noted accordingly, but all other wills must be produced for perusal by the Probate Officer.

Different executors may also be appointed to deal with different parts of the estate. Grants are limited accordingly.

(3) **Grant "save and except".** Probate or administration may be granted of the estate of the deceased, save and except a particular part over which the applicant has no control, or the control of which has been specifically given to some other person.

(4) **Grant Caeterorum.** Where a grant "save and except" part of the property has been made, a grant of the rest (caeterorum) of the estate will be made to the person so entitled.

(5) **Grant to real or personal estate**
Representation may be granted limited to the real estate or to the personal estate (Section 28). In numbers (2), (3), (4) and (5) above an order of the Probate Officer, or of the Court, is necessary.

SPECIAL GRANTS

(1) **Section 31(l)** - issued by order of the Court to a creditor or person interested in the estate where the acting personal representative is residing out of the jurisdiction at the expiration of 12 months from the date of death.

(2) **Section 27 (4)** - gives the High Court complete discretion to appoint anyone to administer the estate of a deceased person where it considers it necessary or expedient to do so. Apart from referring to the Court order, there is no necessity to make any other title in the Oath and Bond. The Circuit Court may make an order under Section 27(4) only where there are contentious proceedings in that Court.

(3) **Illegitimate child.** Where the mother or child (as the case may be) succeeds to the other's estate under Section 9 of the Legitimacy Act 1931, an application must be made to the Probate Officer for an order that a grant issue to the proposed applicant pursuant to Order 79 r.5(1)(c)+(e). Only for deaths before 14/6/1988.

(4) **Adopted child.** Section 3 of the Status of Children Act 1987 provides that the estate devolves as if an adopted child were the legitimate child of the adoptive parents. An application must be made to the Probate Officer for an order that a grant issue to the proposed applicant 0.79 r.5(5).

(5) **Creditors Grant**. Issues pursuant to Court or Probate Officer's Order made under 0 79 r.5(4). It is desirable to serve a citation first on those entitled to apply for a grant. When applying in the Probate Office or District Registry pursuant to the Order all the usual papers are filed but a special Pro Rata Bond (obtainable free from the Probate Office) must be used.

CHAPTER 7

SECOND OR SUBSEQUENT GRANTS

There are several different kinds viz.

1. Administration Intestate de bonis non

Issued when the administrator of an estate dies leaving assets of the deceased unadministered. The grant is given to another party equally entitled or, if none, to the next person entitled. For title, see Chapter 5 and Appendix (No. 21).

2. Administration with Will Annexed de bonis non

If the first grant was a Grant of Probate and the acting executor has died, and all other executors have either died or renounced, Admon. W.A., d.b.n., will be given to the next person entitled. Similarly, if first Grant was Admon. W.A. For title, see Chapter 4 and Appendix (No. 21).

3. Unadministered Probate

Where an executor extracts a Grant of Probate, reserving the rights of another executor and subsequently dies, a Grant of Unadministered Probate will be given to the executor whose rights were reserved.

4. Double Probate

Where an executor extracts a Grant of Probate, reserving the rights of another executor, such other executor may extract a Grant *while the first executor is still alive,* and this Grant is called a Grant of Double Probate.

5. Supplemental Probate

If a Will has been proved by an *executor,* and subsequently, a codicil is discovered, a supplemental Grant of Probate will issue to the acting executor.

6. **Miscellaneous Grants where**, for example,
   (a) a minor attains his majority and applies for a second Grant;
   (b) a donor of a power of attorney applies for a second Grant in his own name;
   (c) a person of unsound mind recovers and applies for a second Grant.

Practice

(a) The second Grant must be applied for in the same Probate Registry from which the first grant issued. But if the primary Grant issued prior to 1/1/1967, all subsequent Grants must be extracted from the Probate Office.

(b) There are no special de bonis non Probate forms. The usual forms must be adapted by inserting the word "unadministered" where appropriate.

(c) A special form of Inland Revenue Affidavit (Form A.3) must be completed.

(d) The first Grant (or an official copy, if it is not available) must be lodged with the application.

(e) The issue of the first Grant and the reason why, and date when, it terminated must be recited in the Oath.

(f) Only the unadministered part of the estate is accounted for in the documents.

(g) A certificate of delay is never required.

(h) An affidavit of due execution of a Will is never required, as it has already been admitted to proof.

(i) There are fixed (low) Probate fees.

(j) If there is a will involved, either an official copy of the will or the original grant of representation may be exhibited in the Oath.

Chain of executorship. Up to 1/1/1967 the acting executor of the sole or surviving executor was entitled to administer the assets of the original testator without extracting a new grant, and this "chain of executorship" could be carried on ad infinitum.

Under Section 19 of the Succession Act, however, where the sole or last surviving executor of a testator dies *after the commencement of the Act,* the executor of such executor shall not be the executor of that testator.

CHAPTER 8

REVOCATION OF GRANTS.
(Sections 26 & 35)

If a grant of representation contains a fundamental error which cannot be corrected by amendment, it must be revoked e.g.

1. Where a grant of administration intestate issues while a valid Will of the deceased is in existence;
2. Where a later Will than that proved has been discovered;
3. Where a Codicil has been discovered which alters the appointment of the executors in the Will;
4. Where one of two or more acting executors has become a person of unsound mind;
5. Where a grant issues after the death of the grantee;
6. Where a person with a prior right to the grantee is discovered;
7. Where the surname or first name of the deceased is totally incorrect;
8. Where the address of the deceased is totally incorrect;
9. Where a grant is made to a person under 18 years of age;
10. Where a grant is made to a person on the basis he was legitimate when, in fact, he is illegitimate;
11. Where a grant has been made to an unmarried woman who erroneously claimed that she was the lawful widow of the deceased;
12. Where a grant has been made in the estate of a living person;
13. Where a grant has been obtained by fraud;
14. Where the Court of Chancery construes a Will differently from the Probate Office and thereby affects title.

Practice

If the grant was obtained by fraud, or if the validity of the will proved is challenged, the grant can be revoked only by a Court order, made in an action or, on consent, on motion before the Probate Judge. In all other cases the grant may be revoked by the Probate Officer. See Appendix (No. 29).

An application to the Probate Officer to revoke must be made in the Registry from which the grant issued and must be grounded on an affidavit referring to any necessary documents e.g. Wills or Certificates. The application should be made by the grantee; if not, the applicant must have the consent of the grantee (unless this is impossible). The original grant must be lodged with the application.

AMENDMENT OF GRANTS

Minor errors, which do not go to the root of a grant, may be rectified by amendment of the grant e.g.

1. Slight misspelling in surname or Christian name e.g. BROWN to BROWNE or ANN to ANNE
2. Adding alternative name or alternative address of deceased or grantee
3. Slight error in address of deceased or grantee
4. Error or omission in description of deceased or grantee
5. Error in place of death
6. Error in date of death
7. Error in the capacity in which the grantee takes the grant (although this may also call for revocation)
8. Misdescription of relationship of grantee to deceased
9. Omission e.g. limitations, or notations re orders made, domicile, etc.

Practice

Affidavit must be made by the grantee exhibiting any necessary certificates, orders, etc., and lodged with the original grant in the Registry from which the grant issued. The Probate Officer will then make an order to amend. See Appendix (No. 28).

IMPOUNDING GRANTS

Grants are impounded:

(1) When the sole executor or administrator becomes insane;

(2) When an intending administrator is unable to obtain justifying surety for his bond - usually because there is contention with the possibility of an administration suit.

CHAPTER 9

CAVEATS, WARNINGS AND APPEARANCES
(0.79, rr. 42-51 inc. - Appendix Q, Forms 20-22, inc.)

A Caveat is a written notice to the Court that nothing be done in regard to the estate of a deceased person unknown to the party entering the Caveat or to his solicitor. It may be entered in the Probate Office or in any District Probate Registry. The effect of a Caveat is to prevent the issue of a grant of representation in that particular estate.

A warning directs the Caveator to enter an appearance to the warning within fourteen days, setting forth his interest and that in default of his doing so the Caveat will cease to have any effect. All Caveats must be warned from the Probate Office. Four copies of the warning must be brought to the Probate Office, including a copy which must be served on the Caveator on the day it is signed by the Probate Officer or on the following day. A Caveat may be warned any time within six months of its lodgment.

An appearance may be entered to the warning within fourteen days after service.

REASONS FOR ENTERING A CAVEAT

(a) To enable the Caveator to make some enquiries to ascertain his position vis-a-vis the estate;
(b) To have some question arising out of the issue of a grant decided by the Court;
(c) To issue a summons to prove a will in solemn form of law;
(d) To issue a citation;
(e) To see that security is sufficient.

HOW TO DISPOSE OF CAVEATS

1. By lapse of time (6 months), if not warned;
2. By voluntary withdrawal by the Caveator (in the Registry where it was entered);
3. By order of Court setting it aside, particularly in intestacy cases;
4. By proving Will in solemn form of law;
5. By no appearance to warning (Side Bar order). May be obtained from Probate Officer on lodgment of affidavit of service of warning with an averment that no appearance has been entered.
6. By order of the Probate Officer, on consent of all the parties and their solicitors (after warning has been entered).

CITATIONS
(0.79, rr. 52-57 inc., Appendix Q, Forms No. 23-32 inc.)

A person interested in the estate of a deceased may issue a citation, requiring the executor or any other person entitled in priority to a grant, to prove the will where they have failed to do so and will not renounce their rights. Similarly, in cases of intestacy. The various types of citation are set out in Appendix Q, Forms No. 23-32 inc.

Procedure:
1. Enter Caveat.
2. Lodge an affidavit setting out all the circumstances of the case and showing interest, with Probate Officer. If he is satisfied, he will make an order that citation issue. If there is a will involved, the original or a copy should be lodged. See Appendix (No. 26).
3. Produce three copies of the Citation, one of which the Probate Officer will sign. This will be sealed and becomes the original.
4. Serve one copy *personally* showing the original.
5. The person cited may enter an appearance within 8 days (Forms No. 22 and 27, Appendix Q).

6. If no appearance is entered, a Side Bar Order, deeming citee to have renounced, will be made by the Probate Officer, on foot of an affidavit of service and of search in the Rules Office for an appearance.
7. If an appearance is entered, the citing party may obtain a Side Bar Order directing the party cited to extract a grant within 14 days.
8. In default, the Probate Officer will make a Side Bar Order, deeming the citee to have renounced.

Citation to Exhibit an Inventory. (Appendix Q, Form No. 32)
This procedure is adopted by beneficiaries and creditors as a convenient way of ascertaining how the administration of an estate is proceeding. A caveat is not required but, otherwise, the initiating procedure is the same as above.

Subpoenas (0.79 r.58 and Appendix D. Form No. 5)
If the party cited, or any other person, has custody of a will of the deceased it may be necessary to issue a subpoena against him to compel him to lodge the will in the Probate Office. A subpoena issues pursuant to Probate Officer's order, made on foot of a satisfactory affidavit, reciting all the circumstances and showing the applicants interest. It is sealed in the Probate Office. It must be served personally by showing the sealed original and delivering a copy. See Appendix (No. 27).

CHAPTER 10

COURT PROCEDURES

Sometimes it becomes necessary to apply to Court in non-contentious cases. Such applications are heard by the Probate Judge, usually on Mondays. They are made ex-parte or on notice.

Ex-parte applications are made by way of *motion paper* which must be lodged in the Rules Office of the Probate Office at least *two clear days* before the day on which such motion, or application, shall be moved. (0.79 r.89).

Applications on notice are made by way of *notice of motion* which must be served personally at least *four clear days* before the day on which such motion or application shall be moved, unless the notice party is represented by a solicitor, when two clear days notice is sufficient (0.52 r.6). Motions being served personally must be stated to be "at the sitting of the Court".

Practice:
(1) Call to the Probate Office to check date for hearing.
(2) Lodge motion paper or original notice of motion duly stamped in the Rules Office. The document should contain a short statement of the principal facts upon which the application is grounded and conclude with the terms in which the motion is to be made (0.79 r.89).
(3) Lodge the original and one plain copy of the affidavit, or affidavits, grounding the application.
(4) Lodge a plain copy of any will referred to in the application. All original exhibits (which must include a death certificate) are handed up in Court.
(5) A copy of the notice of motion and of any affidavit to be used in support of the motion must be served on each notice party (0.52 r.15).

It is difficult to say what motions should be made ex-parte and what should be made on notice. The only real guide is that anyone, whose rights might be prejudiced by the granting of the order sought, should be on notice.

CASES IN WHICH AN APPLICATION MUST BE MADE TO COURT

(i) Application for a grant under Section 27 (4) of the Succession Act including cases of -
   (a) Creditors, where Probate officer declines to appoint.
   (b) By-passing persons with a prior title.
   (c) Applications by personal representatives of a widow where her intestate husband's estate did not exceed £4000 (for death between 1/6/1954 and 1/1/1967) or £500 (for death prior to that);

(ii) Lost wills, for which the three essential proofs are -
   (a) that the will was duly executed,
   (b) that the original was in existence after the death of the deceased,
   (c) that the copy is authentic;

(iii) Where there are rival applications for a grant; and where objection has been raised to the selection of the Probate Officer under 0.79 r.5(3);

(iv) Leave to presume death for the purpose of extracting a grant;

(v) To admit a will to proof by presumption as to due execution;

(vi) Simultaneous deaths (Section 5). Where the question of survival is material to establishing title to a grant of representation an application must be made to Court;

(vii) To set aside a Caveat, particularly in intestacy cases;

(viii) Application for a grant limited for a particular purpose or to a particular part of the estate; (The Probate Officer can make such Orders in some instances);

(ix) Application for a grant ad colligenda bona;

(x)   Where a person entitled to a general grant administration of the estate of a deceased applies to take a limited grant. (O.79 r.21). Limited means limited to part only of the assets or estate of the deceased. (O.79 r.20).

(xi)   Application for a grant under Section 31 (1) of the Succession Act;

(xii) Application for a grant pendente lite (which can also be made in the proceedings);

(xiii) To assign a bond under Section 34(4).

PROBATE ACTIONS

A probate action is a proceeding commenced by originating summons and seeking (a) to prove a will in solemn form of law or (b) to revoke a grant of representation.

Grounds for challenging a will:

(a) The will was not executed according to the Succession Act;
(b) The testator was not of sound disposing mind;
(c) The testator did not know and approve of the contents of the will;

(The above are known as the three statutory pleas).

(d) The testator was unduly influenced;
(e) Execution of the will was obtained by fraud.

Procedure

(1) A Caveat must be entered in the Probate Office (for High Court action). It is not necessary to enter a Caveat before instituting proceedings in the Circuit Court, but anyone who has entered a Caveat must be made a defendant;

(2) The entry of the Caveat must be endorsed on the plenary summons (High Court) in the Rules Office of the Probate Office;

(3) A plenary summons is issued in the High Court or a testamentary civil bill in the Circuit Court;

(4) An affidavit by the plaintiff verifying the indorsement of claim must be filed (See Appendix No. 32).

(5) An affidavit of scripts must be filed by both the plaintiff and defendant (See Appendix C, Form No. 22 – R.S.C.).

(6) The usual appearances and pleadings are filed;

(7) After the pleadings have been closed an application must be made to the Master. to fix time and mode of trial (High Court).

CHAPTER 11

MISCELLANEOUS

CORRECTIVE AFFIDAVITS

When additional assets are discovered after a grant has issued, or when the assets are re-valued upwards, a corrective affidavit, completed by the grantee, must be filed with the Revenue Commissioners and certified by the Probate Officer or District Probate Registrar. In lieu of an affidavit the Revenue Commissioners may issue a Form B5 to the grantee with a request that it be processed in the same way.

Procedure:
(1) Obtain form of affidavit or Form B5 from the Revenue Commissioners, complete original and copy, and have approved by the Revenue Commissioners.
(2) Produce the following documents in the Probate Office or District Probate Registry from where the grant issued:
(a) Original corrective affidavit,
(b) Completed copy corrective affidavit,
(c) Original grant of Probate or Administration (or official copy),
(d) Bond for at least double the gross additional assets - in administration cases,
(e) Justification of sureties for half the penal sum in administration cases.
(3) Have additional Probate fees assessed and have certificate on original affidavit signed by the Probate Officer or District Probate Registrar. The copy affidavit will be retained in the Registry.
(4) Return the original affidavit to the Revenue Commissioners with the amount of additional tax (if any) payable.

Justification of Sureties. The sureties must justify in half the penal sum appearing in the new bond. If, however, the sureties are the same as those who entered in the original bond they must now justify in a figure to cover the new gross amount of the estate (i.e. the original amount plus the additional assets).

Insurance Company. If the bond is from the same insurance company, which entered into the original bond, a letter must be produced to say that the bonds are cumulative.

Grantee dead. If the grantee is dead, a corrective affidavit cannot be passed, as there is no one privy to the estate. The proper procedure is for someone to extract a de bonis non grant.

COPIES OF DOCUMENTS

After a grant has issued, copies of any of the documents which were lodged may be obtained from the Probate Office or District Probate Registry from which the grant issued. These may be bespoken personally or through the post. The date of death and, if possible, the date of grant should be given with all applications.

Grant. An official copy of a grant (at a special low fee) is sufficient evidence of the grant for any purpose in this jurisdiction. (Section 43(2). If bespoken at the time of lodging the papers, the fee is further reduced. Certified copies, and sealed and certified copies may also issue.

Will. An official, certified, or sealed and certified copy of a Will may also be obtained, as above.

For use abroad sealed and certified copies are generally required. For use in the U.S.A. a further certificate from the Probate Judge, together with authentication by the Dept. of Foreign Affairs and the American Embassy, is required.

Inland Revenue Affidavit. Only attested copies of Inland Revenue Affidavits may issue.

Foreign Copies. Where a grant has been obtained abroad and the deceased had assets in this country, an Irish grant is invariably required. A sealed and certified copy of the will must be obtained from the foreign Court for exhibiting in the Oath, together with a sealed and certified copy of the grant.

RECORDS

Documents are retained in the Probate Office or District Probate Registries for twenty years, only, after the grant issues. Copies of documents over 20 years should be bespoken in the National Archives, Bishop St., Dublin, 8.

Copies of all grants issued and of wills proved in District Probate Registries are also available in the Probate Office (for inspection only) for 20 years.

SEARCHES

Searches may be made in the Probate Office, on payment of the prescribed fee, to ascertain if a grant issued from the Probate Office or from any District Probate Registry. The searcher may inspect any document after the grant has issued, but he may not copy them.

CHAPTER 12

ADMINISTRATION OF ASSETS
(Statutory Provisions)

After the grant of representation has issued it is the responsibility of the personal representative to collect all the assets of the deceased, to discharge the funeral expenses, debts and other liabilities of the estate, to distribute the residue of the estate, either according to the terms of the will or according to statute, giving preference to any legal right (Section 45) and to prepare an Executor's or Administrator's Account.

Collection of the assets. The grant of representation, or an official copy thereof, should be sent for noting to the various institutions (Banks, Post Office, etc.) holding assets of the deceased. They will release, or otherwise deal with, the assets as directed by the personal representative.

PAYMENT OF DEBTS AND DISTRIBUTION OF ASSETS

These are governed by various statutory provisions concerning principally, the order of payment of debts where the estate is insolvent, the order of application of the assets where the estate is solvent, the appropriation of parts of the estate *in specie* and the method of vesting immovable property. Care should always be taken to finalise with the Revenue Commissioners the question of death duties or inheritance tax and also income and any other taxes. See 1st Schedule to Act.

A solvent estate is where the assets of the deceased are sufficient to pay the funeral, testamentary and administration expenses and all other debts and liabilities.

An insolvent estate is where the assets of the deceased are not so sufficient.

Payment of Debts - Insolvent Estate:
1. Funeral, Testamentary & Administration Expenses.
2. Secured Creditors
3. Unsecured Creditors
   (a) **Preferential Debts**
       (i)   Rates and Taxes
       (ii) Wages or salary of a labourer or workman or a clerk or servant due within 4 months of death
       (iii) Social Welfare Contributions
       (iv) National Insurance Contributions. These preferential Debts rank equally and, if necessary, abate equally.
   (b) **Ordinary Debts**

Payment of Debts - Solvent Estate
Order of Application of Assets:
Where the estate is solvent the assets are applied in a particular order, (Section 46 & 1st Schedule), as follows:
(1) Property undisposed of by the will;
(2) The residue;
(3) Property specifically appropriated for the payment of debts;
(4) Property charged with the payment of debts;
(5) Pecuniary legacies;
(6) Specific legacies and devises;
(7) Property appointed by the will under *a* general power;
(8) The order of application may be varied by the will.

Marshalling of assets
Where a particular asset is applied out of order, the person entitled to that asset has the right to have the assets "marshalled" so that he may get full value for his legacy and the burden falls on another legacy which is liable before his own (Section 46(5).

LEGACIES

Legacies are gifts of personal property by will. They are of different kinds.

Specific legacies are gifts of particular things which are distinguishable from all other things e.g. "my horse Oscar." Their advantage is that they are usually the last resort to pay debts. Their disadvantage is that they can be adeemed.

General legacies do not specifically identify the things bequeathed e.g. "£100 to A". Their advantage is that they are not adeemed. Their disadvantage is they must all be exhausted, where there is an insufficiency of assets, before specific legacies are resorted to.

Demonstrative legacies are hybrid e.g. "£100 out of my Government Stock". Their advantages are that they are not adeemed and they do not abate until all the general legacies are exhausted. Their disadvantage is that they abate before specific legacies.

Pecuniary Legacies are essentially a gift of a sum of money.

Ademption: Where a specific thing designated in a will no longer exists, or is not the property of the testator at his death, it is said to be adeemed.

Abatement of dispositions in a will occurs where, after payment of all the debts, there is not enough left to pay all the legacies and devises.

Lapse: If a legatee dies in the lifetime of the testator, the legacy lapses and as a rule, if otherwise undisposed of, falls into the residue.

Exceptions to the doctrine of Lapse:
(1) If the legatee who pre-deceased be a lawful child or other issue of the testator and leaves lawful issue living when the testator dies, the legacy takes effect as if the legatee had died immediately after the death of the testator, unless a contrary intention be shown (Section 98);
(2) Where the will shows a contrary intention;

(3) Where the legacy is in fulfilment of a moral or legal obligation;

(4) Where the gift is to a class;

(5) Where the gift is charitable, and the property can be applied *cy-pres*.

DEVISES

Devises are gifts of land or other realty by will. They may be either Specific (e.g. "my farm in Bohola") or General (e.g. "all my land"). They are subject to Abatement, Ademption and Lapse in the same way as legacies.

STATUTORY NOTICE TO CREDITORS

Before distributing the estate, the personal representative may get statutory protection for himself by advertising for creditors. The usual practice is to advertise twice at intervals of one week in a national (and, if necessary, provincial) newspaper, with the time expiring four weeks after the later insertion (Section 49). See Appendix (No. 22).

Retainer is a right whereby a personal representative, who is himself a creditor of the estate, can pay his own debt before paying other creditors of equal degree. It is not exercisable where the estate is insolvent (Section 46(2)).

Preference is a right whereby the personal representative may prefer one creditor as against another in respect of debts of equal degree (Section 46(2)).

Causes of Action. Personal representatives may sue and be sued under the Civil Liability Act 1961, with limitations (Section 48).

Assent. An assent is the method by which the actual transfer of assets to the persons entitled under a will or an intestacy is carried out by the personal representative. It must be in writing in the case of land & houses but not for movables (Section 52). There are special provisions for registered and unregistered land (Sections 53 & 54). Failure to execute an assent is a serious omission in the administration of estates and often necessitates the extraction of a de bonis non grant.

Appropriation. The personal representative may appropriate any part of the estate (real or personal) in its actual condition or state of investment at the time of appropriation, in or towards satisfaction of any share in the estate (Section 55).

The surviving spouse may require the personal representative in writing to appropriate the family house and household chattels in or towards satisfaction of any shares of the surviving spouse. If such share is less than the value of the house and chattels, the right may also be exercised in respect of the share of any infant for whom the spouse is a trustee. (Section 56).

LEGAL RIGHTS

Where a person dies wholly or partly testate (Section 109) the surviving spouse shall be entitled to

(a) ½ of the estate if there are no children

(b) ⅓ of the estate if there are children (Section 111).

This legal right may be renounced (Section 113).

The spouse may elect to take either his legal right or any devise or bequest in will. (Section 115).

Children may also seek a Court Order that provision should be made for them, where a parent has failed to provide for them what a prudent and just parent should. (Section 117). Application must be made to the Court within 6 months of the raising of representation. See Section 46 of the Family Law (Divorce) Act, 1996.

NOTIFICATION AND EXERCISE OF RIGHTS

It is the duty of the personal representative to notify the spouse in writing of the rights conferred by Sections 56 and 115. The rights are exercisable only within six months of the receipt of the notification or one year from the date of the grant, whichever is the later.

UNWORTHINESS TO SUCCEED

Persons may be excluded from taking any share in the estate

of a deceased, where they have been found guilty of certain offences against the deceased or his family, or where the spouse of the deceased has been guilty of certain matrimonial misconduct (Section 120).

EXECUTOR'S YEAR

The personal representative must distribute the estate as soon after the death as is reasonably practicable, but proceedings against him cannot be brought before the expiration of 12 months from the date of death without leave of the Court. Creditors, however, may sue within the 12 months (Section 62).

WHERE A BENEFICIARY CANNOT BE FOUND

Where a beneficiary cannot be found the personal representative may apply to Court to presume him dead, or he can lodge the amount involved in the Central Office of the High Court with an affidavit under the Trustee Act, 1893 (Orders 73 & 77).

LIMITATION OF ACTIONS

Claims against the estate of a deceased person cannot be brought after six years from the date when the right to receive the share accrued. (Section 126).

Claims to recover interest cannot be brought after three years from the date on which the interest became due (Section 126).

Claims by infants and minors must be brought within three years of their disability ending. (Section 127).

Causes of action which survive against the estate of a deceased — proceedings must be brought at latest within two years of the death. (Section 9 of the Civil Liability Act, 1961).

AN ADMINISTRATION SUIT

This is where the Court is asked to administer the estate of the deceased where problems or disputes have arisen in the course of administration as between creditors, beneficiaries or personal representatives. It is instituted by a Special Summons in the High Court or by an Equity Civil Bill in the Circuit Court.

A CONSTRUCTION SUIT

This is a court action aimed at discovering the meaning of a will, where the sense or intention is not clear. It is instituted by Special Summons in the High Court or by an Equity Civil Bill in the Circuit Court.

FAMILY LAW (DIVORCE) ACT, 1996

Under Section 18(1), subject to the other provisions in the Section, where a divorced spouse dies the other spouse may apply to the High Court or Circuit Court within 6 months of representation being first raised, for an Order that provision may be made for her, or him, out of the estate of the deceased spouse, where it is satisfied proper provision had not been made during the lifetime of the deceased under Sections 13, 14, 15, 16 or 17 of the Act. Surviving spouses who have re-married are excluded. The personal representative must make a reasonable attempt to ensure the surviving spouse is notified of the death; and where any such application is made, must not distribute the estate without leave of the Court until it makes or refuses an Order.

DISCLAIMER ON INTESTACY

Where the estate, or a part thereof, of a person who died intestate is disclaimed, the estate, or part, is distributed as if the person disclaiming had died immediately before the intestate, and, if that person is not the spouse, or a direct lineal ancestor, of the intestate, as if that person had died without leaving issue. See the Family Law (Miscellaneous Provisions) Act, 1997, Section 6. When applying for a grant of representation, based on such disclaimer an original must be exhibited in the Oath, and is retained in the Probate Office or particular District Probate Registry.

STEPS IN ADMINISTERING AN ESTATE

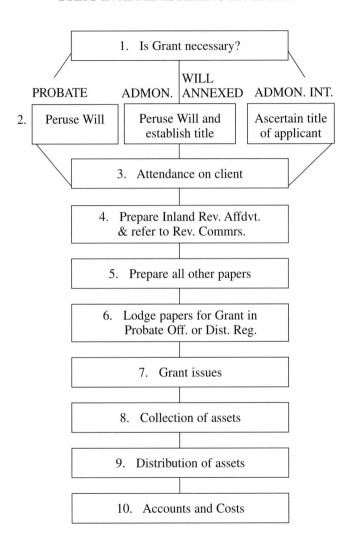

1. Is Grant necessary?

PROBATE   ADMON.   WILL ANNEXED   ADMON. INT.

2. Peruse Will | Peruse Will and establish title | Ascertain title of applicant

3. Attendance on client

4. Prepare Inland Rev. Affdvt. & refer to Rev. Commrs.

5. Prepare all other papers

6. Lodge papers for Grant in Probate Off. or Dist. Reg.

7. Grant issues

8. Collection of assets

9. Distribution of assets

10. Accounts and Costs

APPENDIX

No. l.

HEADING OF FORMS

THE HIGH COURT
PROBATE

The Probate Office/The District Probate Registry at

No. 2.

AFFIDAVIT OF ATTESTING WITNESS

[*Heading as in Form No. 1*].

In the estate of   late of   deceased.

  I,   of
aged eighteen years and upwards *[description]* make oath and
say that I am one of the subscribing witnesses to the last will
[or codicil] of the said
late of *[address and description]* deceased; the said will *[or*
codicil] bearing date the   day of   19
and that the said testator executed the said will *[or* codicil] on
the day of the date thereof, by signing his name *[or* affixing his
mark, being illiterate *or* unable to write from physical debility],
at the foot or end thereof as the same now appears thereon, in
the presence of me and of
the other subscribed witness thereto, both of us being present at
the same time-and we thereupon attested and subscribed the
said will *[or* codicil] in the presence of the said testator and of
each other.
  Sworn, &c.

  NOTE.-The *will* should not be marked by the deponent or by
the commissioner.

ADDITIONS TO THE AFFIDAVIT TO SUIT SPECIAL CIRCUMSTANCES

(a) **Will signed by mark or signature illegible or feeble:** "And I further say that before said testator executed said will [*or* codicil] in manner aforesaid, same was truly, audibly, and distinctly read over to him by me [*or* by X Y in my presence] and said testator appeared fully to understand the same, and was at the time of the execution thereof of sound mind, memory and understanding"

(b) **Blind testator:** Add (a), above, and also the following clause- "And I further say that at the time of execution of said will [*or* codicil] the testator was blind and that I and the said   , the other subscribing witness, signed our names in such a position that had the testator been possessed of his eyesight, he could have seen us so sign"

(c) **Testator signs more than once:** "And I further say that the testator signed his name twice because he had difficulty in signing his name the first time [*or,* as the case may be] but all being done in the one continuous act of execution"

(d) **Unexecuted alterations:** "And, having particularly observed the words '.......' interlined between the [6th] and [7th] lines of the [1st] page of the said will and the alteration of the word '.......' to '........' in the [8th] line of [2nd] page and the erasure over which is written the word '.......' on the [10th] line of the [2nd] page, I further say that the said recited interlineation, alteration and overwritten erasure were written and made in the said will prior to execution thereof"

(e) **Plight and Condition:** "And, having particularly observed that the said will is torn along the left-hand side and that certain pin-holes and clip marks appear at the top left-hand corner, I further make oath and say that I tore the page on which I wrote the will from a double sheet of blank foolscap paper [*or* as the case may be] prior to execution of the said will and that the said pin-holes and clip marks were caused when policies of insurance were attached to the will by the deceased [*or,* as the case may be]. Nothing of a testamentary nature was at any time attached to the said will, which is now, except for the said pin-holes and clip-marks, in the same plight and condition as when executed by the said testator."

No. 3

ADMINISTRATION BOND

[*Heading as in Form No. 1*].

We [*names, addresses and descriptions of administrator and sureties*] are each liable in full to pay to the President of the High Court the sum of   for which payment we bind ourselves and each of us and our

Sealed with our seal [s] and dated the   day of 19
The condition of this obligation is that if the above-named

the   of   late of deceased, and the intended administrator/administratrix of the estate of the said deceased,
do, when lawfully called on in that behalf, make or cause to be made a true inventory of the said estate which has or shall come into his/her hands, possession or knowledge, or into the hands, possession or control of any other person for him/her; do exhibit the said inventory or cause it to be exhibited in the Probate Office [*or* in the district probate registry at   ] whenever required by law to do so; do well and truly administer the said estate according to law, paying all the debts owed by the deceased at the time of his death, all death duties payable in respect of the estate of the deceased for which the personal representative is accountable and all income tax and surtax payable out of the estate,
distributing all shares in the estate to those entitled by law thereto and as the law requires him/her;
and further, do make or cause to be made a true account of the said administration whenever required by law to do so; and further do, if so required, render and deliver up the letters of administration in the High Court if it shall hereafter appear that any will was made by the deceased which is exhibited in the

74

said Court with a request that it be allowed and approved accordingly;

then this obligation shall be void and of no effect, but shall otherwise remain in full force and effect.

Signed, sealed and delivered   SEAL
by the within-named

in the presence of   SEAL

No. 4

ADMINISTRATION (INTESTATE) BOND

[*Heading as in Form No. 1*].

Know all men by these presents that we [*names, addresses and descriptions of administrator and sureties*] are jointly and severally bound unto The Honourable Frederick Morris, President of the High Court in Ireland and his successors in office, in the sum of   Pounds to be paid to the said President or to his said successors, for which payment to be made we bind ourselves and each of us for the whole, our Heirs, Executors, and Administrators, by these presents.

Sealed with our Seals. Dated the   day of in the year of our Lord One thousand nine hundred and

The Condition of this obligation is such that if the above bounden

the   of   late of   deceased, and the intended Administrat   of the estate of the said deceased

do, when lawfully called on in that behalf, make, or cause to be made, a true inventory of the personal estate of the said deceased which has or shall come to h   hands, possession, or knowledge, or into the hands and possession or control of any other person for h   , and also of the Real Estate of the said deceased, devolving to and vesting in h   as legal personal representative of said deceased, and the same so made do exhibit, or cause to be exhibited, into the   Registry at

whenever required by law so to do; and all such Estates and all other such personal and real estates of the said deceased at the time of h   death, which at any time after shall come to the hands, possession or control of the said

or into the hands, possession or control

76

of any other person or persons for h   do well and truly administer according to law [that is to say] do pay the debts which deceased did owe at his decease death duties payable in respect of the estate of said deceased for which the personal representative is accountable, all income tax and surtax payable out of the said estate and as the Law charge h and further, do make, or cause to be made a true account of   said Administration whenever required by law so to do; and all the rest and residue of all such estates and effects to deliver and pay unto such person or persons as shall be entitled thereto, under the Statutes in such case made and provided. And if it shall hereafter appear that any last Will was made by the said deceased, and the executor or executors or other persons therein named do exhibit the same into the said District or Principal Registry making request to have it allowed and approved according, if the said

being thereunto required, do render and deliver the said Letters of Administration granted to

[approbation of such Testament being first had and made], then this obligation to be void and of none effect, or else to remain in full force and virtue.

Signed, sealed and delivered   SEAL
by the said

in the presence of   SEAL

FOR DEATH PRIOR TO 1/6/1959

No. 5

ADMINISTRATION (INTESTATE) BOND

[*Heading as in Form No. 1*].

Know all men by these presents that we [*names, addresses and descriptions of administrator and sureties*] are jointly and severally bound unto The Honorable Frederick Morris President of the High Court in Ireland and his successors in office, in the sum of   Pounds to be paid to the said President or to his said successors, for which payment to be made we bind ourselves and each of us for the whole, our Heirs, Executors, and Administrators, by these presents.

Sealed with our seals. Dated the   day of in the year of our Lord One thousand nine hundred and

The condition of this obligation is such that if the above bounden

the   of   late of   deceased and the intended Administrat   of the personal estate of the said deceased

do, when lawfully called on in that behalf, make, or cause to be made, a true inventory of the personal estate of the said deceased which has or shall come to h hands, possession, or knowledge, or into the hands and possession or control of any other person for h , and also of so much of the Real Estate of the said deceased as shall devolve to and vest in h

as legal personal representative of said deceased, and the same so made do exhibit, or cause to be exhibited, into the Registry at

whenever required by law so to do; and all such Estates, and all other such personal and real estates of the said deceased at the time of h   death, which at any time after shall come to the hands, possession or control of the said

or into the hands, possession or control of any other person or persons for h   do well and truly administer according to law

78

[that is to say] do pay the debts which deceased did owe at his decease and as the Law charge h   ; and further, do make, or cause to be made a true account of   said Administration whenever required by law so to do; and all the rest and residue of all such estates and effects to deliver and pay unto such person or persons as shall be entitled thereto, under the Statutes in such case made and provided. And if it shall hereafter appear that any last Will was made by the said deceased, and the executor or executors or other persons therein named do exhibit the same into the said District or Principal Registry making request to have it allowed and approved accordingly, if the said

being thereunto required, do render and deliver the said Letters of Administration granted to

[approbation of such Testament being first had and made], then this obligation to be void and of none effect, or else to remain in full force and virtue.

Signed, sealed and delivered   SEAL
by the said

in the presence of   SEAL

No. 6

ADMINISTRATION WITH WILL ANNEXED BOND

[*Heading as in Form No. 1*].

Know all men by these presents that we [*names, addresses and descriptions of administrator and sureties*] are jointly and severally bound unto The Honorable Frederick Morris President of the High Court in Ireland and his successors in office, in the sum of   Pounds to be paid to the said President or to his said successors, for which payment to be made we bind ourselves and each of us for the whole, our Heirs, Executors, and Administrators, by these presents.

Sealed with our seals, and dated the   day of in the year of our Lord One thousand nine hundred and

The condition of this obligation is such that if the above bounden
the   of   late of   deceased

the intended Administrat   with the Will dated the day of   annexed of the estate of the said deceased do, when lawfully called on in that behalf make or cause to be made, a true inventory of the personal estate of the said deceased, and also of the Real Estate of the said deceased devolving to and vesting in h as legal personal representative of said deceased which has or shall come to h   hands, possession, control or knowledge and the same so made do exhibit, or cause to be exhibited, into the
Registry at
whenever required by law so to do; and such personal and real estate   do well and truly administer [that is to say] do pay the debts of the said deceased which he did owe at his decease death duties payable in respect of the estate of said

80

deceased for which the personal representative is accountable all income tax and surtax payable out of the said estate and then the legacies contained in the said Will annexed to the said Letters of Administration, so to h committed as far as the said personal and real estate will thereto extend, and as the law charge h and further, do make, or cause to be made, a true account of h said Administration when he shall be thereunto lawfully required, and all the residue of the said personal and real estate shall deliver and pay unto such person or persons as shall be by law entitled thereto, then this obligation to be void and of none effect, or else to remain in full force and virtue.

Signed, sealed and delivered   SEAL
by the said

in the presence of   SEAL

FOR DEATH PRIOR TO 1/6/1959

No. 7

ADMINISTRATION WITH WILL ANNEXED BOND

[*Heading as in Form No. 1*].

Know all men by these presents that we [*names, addresses and descriptions of administrator and sureties*] are jointly and severally bound unto The Honorable Frederick Morris President of the High Court in Ireland and his successors in office, in the sum of   Pounds to be paid to the said President or to his said successors, for which payment to be made we bind ourselves and each of us for the whole, our Heirs, Executors, and Administrators, by these presents.

Sealed with our seals, and dated the   day of in the year of our Lord One thousand nine hundred and

The condition of this obligation is such that if the above bounden the   of   late of   deceased, the intended Administrat   with the Will dated the day of   annexed, of all the personal estate of the said deceased do, when lawfully called on in that behalf, make, or cause to be made, a true inventory of the personal estate of the said deceased, and also of so much of the Real Estate of the said deceased as shall devolve to and vest in h   as legal personal representative of said deceased which has or shall come to h hands, possession, control or knowledge and the same so made do exhibit, or cause to be exhibited, into the   Registry at whenever required by law so to do; and such personal and real estate   do well and truly administer [that is to say] do pay the debts of the said deceased which he did owe at his decease, and then the legacies contained in the said Will annexed to the said Letters of Administration, so to h committed as far as the said personal and real estate will thereto extend, and as the law charge h   and further, do

82

make, or cause to be made, a true account of h   said
Administration when he shall be thereunto lawfully required,
and all the residue of the said personal and real estate shall
deliver and pay unto such person or persons as shall be by law
entitled thereto, then this obligation to be void and of none
effect, or else to remain in full force and virtue.

Signed, sealed and delivered   SEAL
by the said

in the presence of   SEAL

No. 8

AFFIDAVIT OF MARKET VALUE

[Heading as in Form No. 1]

In the estate of   late of   deceased

I,   of   in the County of
[Occupation]   aged 18
years and upwards, make Oath and say as follows:

(1)   I am acquainted with the value of lands in the vicinity
of   in the County of
where land/s belonging to the said   deceased
is/are situate.

(2)   I have inspected the holding of deceased at
and in my opinion the said holding would, on the date of the
swearing hereof, have been of the value of about
Pounds if then offered for sale in open market.

Sworn,&c.

NOTE.-*This Affidavit may be made by any auctioneer,
professional valuer, practical farmer or chartered surveyor.*

No. 9

RENUNCIATION OF ADMINISTRATION

[Heading as in Form No. 1].

In the estate of   Whereas
late of   late of   deceased
                    deceased.   died a bachelor and intestate
on the   day of   19   , at [*where application
is made to a District Probate Registry, add* having *at* the time
of his death *a* fixed place of abode at   within the
district of   ] And whereas, I   of   am his
[*state relationship*]

Now I, the said   aged eighteen years and
upwards, do hereby renounce all my rights to letters of
administration of the   estate of the said deceased.

                    Dated
                    (Signed)
Witness

84

No. 10

RENUNCIATION OF PROBATE OR ADMINISTRATION WITH THE WILL ANNEXED

[*Heading as in Form No. 1*].

In the estate of   Whereas
late of   late of
                  deceased.   deceased, died on the
                                          day of   19   , at
[*where application is made in a District Probate Registrar, add*
having at the time of his death a fixed place of abode at
                                    within the district of   ]
and whereas, he made and duly executed his last will [*or* will
and   codicils] bearing date the   day of
19   , and thereof appointed   executor [*or as
the case may be*] .

   Now I, the said   aged eighteen years
and upwards, do declare that I have not intermeddled with the
                  estate of the said deceased, and will not
hereafter intermedddle therein, with the intent to defraud
creditors, and I do hereby expressly renounce my right to
probate of the said will [*or* will and codicils], [*or* to letters of
administration with the said will [*or* will and codicils] annexed]
of the   estate of the said deceased.

                  Dated
                  (Signed)
Witness

STATUS OF CHILDREN ACT, 1987

The Status of Children Act, 1987, applies to all Wills made on, or after, the 14th June, 1988, and to all deaths intestate on or after that date.

Section 3 provides that the relationship between every person and his father and mother shall be determined irrespective of whether his father and mother are, or have been, married to each other, and *all other relationships shall be determined accordingly.*

Under Section 27, any reference in a Will to issue or child now includes non-marital children, unless the contrary intention appears.

Under Section 29 non-marital children have equal succession rights to the estates of all their blood relations and vice versa. It also sets up a rebuttable presumption that a child, whose parents have not married each other, and who dies intestate, is not survived by his father or by any person related to him through his father.

Section 30 deals with applications for Grants of Probate and administration. It sets up a rebuttable presumption that where a non-marital relationship affects the title to a Grant, all those persons who would be entitled to apply for a Grant on the basis of that non-marital relationship have predeceased the deceased.

Intestate titles:

(a) a bachelor without parent - there is no necessity to clear off the possibility that an unmarried person might have had issue:

(b) a bachelor and that I am the lawful son —

Proofs for Probate Officer:

The long form of birth certificate must be exhibited in the Oath for Administrator. Where a mother and non-marital child are involved this is accepted as conclusive. Where a father and non-marital child are involved Section 46(3) presumes the father registered on the birth certificate to be the father of the child unless the contrary is proved on the balance of probabilities. If the father's name does not so appear, an application may be made exparte to the Probate Officer in his list. If he is not convinced, an application will have to be made to Court. A declaration of parentage may be sought from the Circuit Court under Section 35.

POWER OF ATTORNEY FOR ADMINISTRATION W.A.
on behalf of the Executor

[Heading as in Form No. 1].

Whereas A.B., late of   , in the county of *[Description]*, deceased, died on the   day of
19 having made and duly executed his last will and testament *[and codicil, in any]* , and therein appointed C.D. sole executor.

Now I, the said C.D., being of the age of eighteen years and upwards, and at present residing at
do hereby nominate, constitute and appoint X.Y., of   ,
in the county of   , Ireland, to be my true and lawful attorney, to apply in the High Court for letters of administration with the said will annexed of the estate of the said A.B., deceased, for my use and benefit and until I shall apply for and obtain probate of said will, and for that purpose to do all lawful acts and deeds which may be deemed necessary or advisable in the matter of the said estate, I hereby undertaking to ratify and confirm all lawful acts done by the said X.Y. on my behalf with regard to the taking out of such letters of administration with said will annexed of the said estate of the said A.B., deceased.

Dated the   day of   19

Signed and delivered by the
said C.D., in presence of

Witness

POWER OF ATTORNEY FOR ADMINISTRATION INTESTATE

[Heading as in Form No. 1].

Whereas A.B., late of   ,   in   the   county   of *[Description]*,   deceased,   died   intestate   a   widower   on   the   day of   , 19   , leaving me C.D., his lawful son and next-of-kin him surviving.

Now I, the said C.D., at present residing at and being of the age of eighteen years and upwards, do hereby nominate, constitute and appoint X.Y., of   , in   the   County of   Ireland, to be my true and lawful attorney to   apply   in   the   High   Court   in   Ireland   for   letters   of administration of the estate of the said A.B., deceased, for my use and benefit and until I myself shall apply for and obtain letters of administration of the estate of the said, A.B., deceased and for that purpose to do all lawful acts and deeds which may be   deemed   necessary   or   advisable   in   the   matter   of   the   said estate, I hereby undertaking to ratify and confirm all lawful acts done by the said X.Y. on my behalf with regard to the taking out of   such   letters   of   administration   of   the   said   estate   of   the   said A.B., deceased.

Dated the   day of   19

Signed and delivered by the
said C.D., in presence of

Witness

No. 14

(a) SHARES ON INTESTACY FOR DEATH ON OR SINCE 1/1/1967

Relative surviving	Distribution of estate
Husband and issue	Two-thirds to husband; one-third equally among children, with issue of predeceased child taking *per stirpes*
Widow and issue	Two-thirds to widow; one third equally among children with issue of predeceased child taking *per stirpes*
Husband and no issue	Husband takes all
Widow and no issue	Widow takes all
Issue and no spouse	Children take equally, with issue of predeceased child taking *per stirpes*
Father, mother, brothers and sisters	Each parent takes one-half
Father, brothers and sisters	Father takes all
Mother, brothers and sisters	Mother takes all
Brothers and sisters	All take equally. Children of predeceased brother or sister take *per stirpes*
Nephews and nieces and grandparent	Nephews and nieces take all equally

see over

Nephews and nieces, uncles and aunts and great grandparents	Nephews and nieces take all equally
Uncles and aunts and great grandparents	Uncles and aunts take all equally
First cousin, great uncle, great nephew and great great grandparent	First cousin, great uncle and great nephew take all equally

NOTE.-See section headed "Parties entitled in Distribution" in Chapter 5 for definition and scope of *per stirpes* doctrine. The above rules apply to all property both real and personal.

No. 14

(b) SHARES ON INTESTACY FOR DEATH
PRIOR TO 1/1/1967

Relative surviving	Distribution of estate
Husband and issue	Husband took whole estate
Widow and issue	One-third to widow; two-thirds equally among children, with issue of predeceased child taking *per stirpes*
Husband and no issue	Husband took whole estate
Widow and no issue	Widow took first £4000 and half of remainder. Other half to next-of-kin in equal shares; if there were none, then to widow
Issue and no spouse	Children took equally, with issue of predeceased child taking *per stirpes*
Father, mother, brothers and sisters	Father took whole estate
Father, brothers and sisters	Father took whole estate
Mother, brothers and sisters	All took equally. Children of predeceased brother or sister took *per stirpes*
Brothers and sisters	All took equally. Children of predeceased brother or sister took *per stirpes*
Nephews and nieces and grandparent	Grandparent took all

see over

Nephews and nieces, uncles and aunts and great grandparents	All took equally
Uncles and aunts and great grandparents	All took equally
First cousin, great uncle, great nephew and great great grandparent	All took equally

NOTE.-The rules prior to 1/1/1967 applied only to personal property. Real property descended to the heir-at-law, except freehold registered land, which, under Part IV of the 1891 Act, was distributed as personalty.

INTESTATE SUCCESSION FOR DEATHS ON OR AFTER 1/1/1967 AND ORDER OF ENTITLEMENT TO GRANT

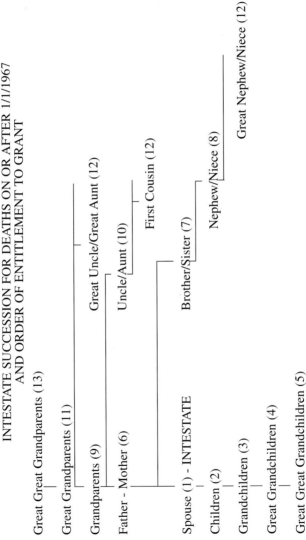

Great Great Grandparents (13)

Great Grandparents (11)

Grandparents (9)

Great Uncle/Great Aunt (12)

Father - Mother (6)

Uncle/Aunt (10)

First Cousin (12)

Brother/Sister (7)

Nephew/Niece (8)

Great Nephew/Niece (12)

Spouse (1) - INTESTATE

Children (2)

Grandchildren (3)

Great Grandchildren (4)

Great Great Grandchildren (5)

SPECIMEN TITLES-ADMINISTRATION INTESTATE
(Death on, or after, 1/1/1967)

Husband or widow	I am the lawful husband/widow.
Child of married man	Died a married man leaving him surviving his widow, A, who has since died *or* who has duly renounced her rights [*exhibit renunciation*] and I am the lawful son/daughter.
Child of married woman	Died a married woman leaving her surviving her lawful husband, B, who .... (as above).
Child of widow or widower	Died a widow/widower and I am the lawful son/daughter.
Grandchild	Died a widow/widower without child her/him surviving and that 1 am the lawful grandchild.
Father or Mother	Died a bachelor [*or* a widower without child, grandchild or other descendant] and that 1 am the lawful father/mother.
Brother or Sister	Died a bachelor [*or* widower, etc.] without parent and that I am the lawful brother/sister.
Nephew or Niece	Died a bachelor [*or* widower, etc.] without parent, brother or sister and that I am the lawful nephew/ niece.
Grandparent	A bachelor [*or* widower, etc.] without parent, brother or sister, nephew or niece and that I am the lawful grandfather/grandmother.

Uncle or Aunt	A bachelor [*or* widower, etc.] without parent, brother or sister, nephew or niece or grandparent and that I am the lawful uncle/ aunt.
First Cousin	A bachelor [*or* widower, etc.] without parent, brother or sister, nephew or niece, grandparent, uncle or aunt or great grandparent and that I am the lawful first cousin.
First Cousin once removed	A bachelor [*or* widower, etc.] without parent or other lineal ancestor brother or sister, nephew or niece or descendant of such, uncle or aunt in any degree or first cousin and that 1 am the lawful first cousin once removed.

No. 17

PARTIES ENTITLED IN DISTRIBUTION

Issue of predeceased child	A married man leaving him surviving his widow, A, who has since died and one lawful and only child, B., who has duly renounced his rights [*exhibit renunciation*] and that I am the lawful son/daughter of C who was a lawful child of and who predeceased the deceased.
Issue of predeceased brother or sister	A bachelor [*or* widower, etc.] without parent leaving one lawful and only brother A, and one lawful and only sister B., both of whom have since died and that I am the lawful son/daughter of C who was a lawful brother/sister of and who predeceased the deceased.

95

REPRESENTATIVE OF NEXT-OF-KIN

Representative of child	A widow without grandchild or other descendant who would have been the issue of a predeceased child and leaving her surviving two lawful and only children A, who has since died and B, who has duly renounced her rights [*exhibit renunciation*] and that I am the personal representative of the said A, under a grant of Probate which issued to me on the day of 19 from the....
Representative of brother or sister	A bachelor without parent or nephew or niece who would have been the issue of a predeceased brother or sister and leaving her surviving one lawful and only brother A, and two lawful and only sisters, B and C, all of whom have since died and that I am the personal representative of the said A, under a grant of Letters of Administration Intestate which issued to me on the day of 19 from the...

SPES SUCCESSIONIS

To brother or sister, father renouncing and consenting

A bachelor *[or* widower, etc.] without mother, leaving him surviving his lawful father, A, who has duly renounced his rights and consented hereto *[exhibit renunciation]* and that I am the lawful son/daughter of the said A.

No. 20.

SPECIMEN TITLES-ADMINISTRATION WITH WILL ANNEXED

(Death on, or after, 1/1/1967)

(a) No executor appointed	(a) — and that he did not therein name any executor *and that I am the Residuary Legatee and Devisee named in said will*
(b) Executor dead	(b) — and that he did therein name as sole executor XY, who predeceased the deceased *or who survived the deceased and has since died without proving said will and that I am the Residuary Legatee and Devisee named in said will*
(c) Executor renounces	(c) — and that he did therein name as sole executor XY *who has duly renounced his rights upon which renunciation dated... . I have signed my name and that I am the Residuary Legatee and Devisee named in said will*
(d) No executor appointed and residue not disposed of	(d) — and that he did not therein name any executor or Residuary Legatee and Devisee *and that I am the widow of the said deceased*
(e) No executor appointed and Residuary Legatee and Devisee renounces	(e) — and that he did not therein name any Executor but did therein name as Residuary Legatee and Devisee XY who has duly renounced his rights *[exhibit renunciation]* and *that I am a legatee named in said will*

98

(f) No executor appointed and Residuary Legatee and Devisee survived and died

— and that he did not therein name any executor but did therein name as Residuary Legatee and Devisee XY, who survived the deceased and has since died *and that I am the personal representative of the said XY under grant of Admon. Int. which issued to me from the Probate Office on the   day of*

(g) Executor, Residuary Legatee and Devisee predeceased

— and that he did therein name as sole executor, Residuary Legatee and Devisee XY who predeceased the deceased *and that I am the widow of said deceased*

(h) Attorney of executor

— and did therein name as sole executor AB who is aged eighteen years and upwards and is now residing at *[Give address abroad in full] [Description]* that I am the attorney lawfully appointed of the said AB under power of attorney dated   upon which I have signed my name

SPECIMEN TITLES-ADMINISTRATION INTESTATE
de bonis non (Death on, or after 1/1/1967)

1. died Intestate [*a married man*] leaving him surviving his widow, A, who extracted a Grant of Letters of Administration Intestate from the Probate Office on the 21st February 1972 and died on the 6th June 1979 leaving part of the estate of said deceased unadministered that I am the lawful son of the said deceased.

2. died Intestate a Bachelor without parent and that on the 18th March 1969 a Grant of Letters of Administration Intestate issued forth of the Cork District Probate Registry to A, his lawful brother who died on the 11th November 1978 leaving part of the said estate unadministered that I am the lawful sister of the said deceased.

SPECIMEN TITLES-ADMINISTRATION W.A., de bonis non
(Death on, or after 1/1/1967)

1. and did therein name as his sole executor A who extracted a Grant of Probate from the Probate Office on the   and died on the
    leaving part of the estate of said deceased unadministered, and that I am the Residuary Legatee and Devisee named in the said Will

2. and did not therein name any executor but did therein name as Residuary Legatee and Devisee A who extracted a Grant of Administration W.A. from the Probate Office on the   and died on the
    leaving part of the estate of said deceased unadministered, and that I am the personal representative of the said A under a Grant Admon. Int. which issued to me from the Probate Office on the

No. 22

STATUTORY NOTICE TO CREDITORS

In the estate of   late of   in the

NOTICE

Notice is hereby given pursuant to Section 49 of the Succession Act 1965 that particulars in writing of all claims against the estate of the above named deceased who died on the
day of   19   (Probate of whose will was granted to the Executors on the   day of   19   ) should be furnished to the undersigned solicitors for the Executors on or before the day of 19 after which date the assets will be distributed having regard only to the claims furnished.

Dated the   day of   19

Murphy & Co.,
Solicitors,
4, Arab Street,
Dublin, 2.

No. 23

AFFIDAVIT OF MENTAL CAPACITY BY DOCTOR

[heading as in Form No. 1].

In the estate of   late of   in the
County of   deceased

I,   of
in the County of   ,
Medical Practitioner, aged 18 years and upwards make oath and say as follows: '

1.   I attended the above-named   in my professional capacity for a period of ten years between 1967 and 1977. I am informed and believe that he made his last Will on the 29th October 1970. I am quite satisfied that he was of sound disposing mind on that date and fully capable of making his Will.

Sworn etc.

AFFIDAVIT OF MENTAL CAPACITY BY SOLICITOR

[Heading as in Form No. 1].

In the estate of   late of   in the
County of   deceased

I   of   in
the County of

Solicitor, aged 18 years and upwards make oath and say as follows:

1. I knew the above-named   for upwards of 20 years prior to his death on the 20th November 1977. During that period he frequently consulted me about his affairs.

2. On the 20th October 1960 he called to my office for the purpose of making his Will. I found him lucid and fully capable of discussing all his affairs and giving me instructions for drawing his Will. I am quite satisfied that he had full testamentary capacity at that time.

3. At the time he made his Will the said   was engaged actively in farming his land at
He continued to do so up until July 1977 when he was admitted to the Mental Hospital in   because of senility and because there was no-one to look after him. He died in the said Mental Hospital on the 19th October 1977.

4. As far as I have been able to ascertain the doctor who was attending the said   about the time he made his Will was   of
who died on the 30th November last.

Sworn, &c.

No. 25

AFFIDAVIT OF IDENTITY OF EXECUTOR

[Heading as in Form No. 1].

In the estate of AB late of   in the
County of   deceased

I, John Magee, of Trout Street, Wexford in the County of Wexford, Carpenter, aged eighteen years and upwards, make oath and say as follows:

1. The above-named AB died on the 12th day of June 1976 having made and duly executed his last will on the 6th day of May 1974, wherein he appointed "Sonny Magee of Trout Street Wexford" to be his executor.

2. At the date of the said Will there was no person bearing the surname of Magee living at Trout Street aforesaid other than myself, this deponent and my wife Mary.

3. I was living at the said address at the date of the Will, and I am popularly known as "Sonny" Magee, by which name the said deceased always addressed me.

4. I further make oath and say that the said deceased informed me some time previously to his death that he had appointed me as his executor, and that I am the person called Sonny Magee.

John Magee

Sworn, &c.

No. 26

AFFIDAVIT TO LEAD TO A CITATION

[Heading as in Form No. 1].

In the estate of AB late of   in the
County of   deceased

I, CD of   *[Description]* aged eighteen years and upwards made oath and say as follows:

1. The above-named AB late of   in the County of   , Farmer, died on or about the day of   having duly executed his last will on the day of   . I beg to refer to a copy of said will when produced.

2. In his said will the said testator did therein name FE of   as sole executor and Residuary Legatee and Devisee and bequeathed a sum of five thousand pounds to me.

3. The said FE has neglected or refused to extract a grant of Probate of said will as a result of which I have been unable to obtain my said bequest.

4. By letters dated the   day of   my solicitors, Messrs. XY, have requested the said FE to extract a grant of Probate of the said will. I beg to refer to copies of the said letters when produced. No reply has been received to any of said letters.

5. I am desirous, therefore, that a citation should issue against the said FE to accept or refuse a grant of Probate of said will.

Sworn, &c.

No. 27

AFFIDAVIT TO LEAD TO A SUBPOENA

[Heading as in Form No. 1].

In the estate of AB late of   in the
                    County of   deceased

I, CD of   , Dublin, *[Description]* aged
eighteen years and upwards, make oath and say as follows:

1. The above-named AB late of   in the
    County of   , died at the   Dublin
    on or about the 15th day of March 1978 having previously
    thereto, as I believe, duly made and executed his last will
    and testament and thereof made me his residuary legatee
    and devisee.

2. I desire to have the said will proved but the same has been
    since said deceased's death, and now remains, as I verily
    believe, in the custody and possession of Messrs. XY,
    Solicitors, of   , Dublin.

3. I have by letter from my solicitors, Messrs. Jones, dated
    the 6th day of June 1978 requested said Messrs. XY to
    deliver the said Will to me or to lodge it in the Probate
    Office, but they have refused or declined to do either. I beg
    to refer to a copy of said letter when produced.

4. I therefore pray a subpoena to issue against the said
    Messrs. XY requiring them to bring into and leave in the
    Probate Office the said Will.

    Sworn, &c.

No. 28

AFFIDAVIT TO LEAD TO AMENDMENT OF GRANT

[Heading as in Form No. 1].

In the estate of AB late of   in the
County of   deceased

I, XY of   in the County of
[Description] aged eighteen years and upwards make oath and
say as follows:

1. On the 25th day of September 1978 a Grant of Probate of
    the last Will of AB late of   aforesaid   issued
    forth of the   District Probate Registry to me, this
    deponent, the sole executor named therein.

2. The date of death of said deceased, as it appears in the
    said Grant of Probate, is the 17th day of April 1978,
    whereas the correct date of death was the 7th day of
    April 1978. I beg to refer to the death certificate of the
    said deceased upon which marked with the latter "A"
    I have endorsed my name prior to the swearing hereof.

3. The error in the date was not observed by me when the
    Oath of Executor was read over to me with the incorrect
    date inadvertently inserted therein.

4. I desire that the said Grant of Probate be amended by
    altering the date of death to read the 7th day of April
    1978.

    Sworn, &c.

No. 29

AFFIDAVIT TO LEAD TO REVOCATION OF GRANT

[Heading as in Form No. 1].

In the estate of   late of   deceased

I,   of   in the County of
[Description] aged eighteen years and upwards, make oath and say as follows:

1. The above-named   late of
    Dublin, died a Widower on the   day of   1978 and a
    Grant of Letters of Administration Intestate of his estate
    issued to me from the Probate Office on the   day of
    1978, as his lawful son.

2. I verily believed at the time I swore the Oath of
    Administration that the deceased had died intestate. I had
    been living in Cork for many years and though I visited my
    father from time to time he rarely mentioned his personal
    affairs to me and at no time mentioned that he had drawn a
    Will. I searched diligently through his papers after his
    death and also enquired from his solicitors but did not find
    any trace of a Will.

3. Subsequent to the issue of the said Grant to me, it came to
    my notice that my father had lodged some documents
    for safekeeping in the   Branch at   , Dublin.
    On inspecting these documents I discovered a Will of my
    late father executed on the 1st day of April 1967. I beg to
    refer to the said Will when produced.

4. I am therefore desirous that the said Grant of Letters of
    Administration Intestate of the said estate of the said
    deceased granted to me as aforesaid should be revoked and
    cancelled.

    Sworn, &c.

No. 30

ELECTION OF A GUARDIAN BY INFANTS

[Heading as in Form No. 1].

In the estate of   Whereas
late of   late of   deceased
         deceased.   died a widower and intestate
on the   day of   19 , at
[where application is made in a District Probate Registry, add
having at the time of his death a fixed place of abode at
within the district of   ], leaving   his natural
and lawful and only children, the said   being an
infant of the age of   years only, the said   being
also an infant of the age of   years only.

Now we the said   and
do hereby make choice of and elect
our lawful maternal uncle [*or as the case may be*] and one of
our next-of-kin to be our guardian for the purpose of his
obtaining letters of administration of the   estate of
the said   deceased, to be granted to him for our use
and until one of us shall attain the age of eighteen years, and
shall apply for and obtain letters of administration of the
said   estate, or until all of us shall attain the age
of eighteen [*or* for the purpose of renouncing for us, and on our
behalf all our right, title, and interest to and in the letters of
administration, &c., [*as the case may be*], [*add in cases where
a solicitor appears for the infants*] and we hereby
appoint   of   our
solicitor to file or cause to be filed this our election for us in the
Probate Office [*or* District Probate Registry at   ]

Dated

(Signed)

Witness

No. 31

PETITION TO BE APPOINTED GUARDIAN OF INFANTS

[Heading as in Form No. 1].

The petition of AB the natural and lawful maternal uncle of X, Y and Z, infants, the natural and lawful children and only next-of-kin of CD late of   in the County of   deceased, intestate

Sheweth—

That the said CD died on or about the   day of   19   , intestate, a widower, leaving him surviving the said infants, his natural and lawful children and only next-of-kin.

That the said infants are of the ages following, that is to say, the said X aged   years, the said Y aged   years and the said Z aged   years, and by reason thereof are incapable by law to take upon themselves letters of administration of the estate of the said deceased.

That there is no testamentary or other lawfully appointed guardian of the said infants.

That the said infants have no grandparent them surviving. That the said infants by form of election duly executed have consented that the said letters of administration should be granted to your petitioner for their use and benefit.

That the said infants live and reside at   aforesaid and said place is distant from your petitioner not more than   miles.

That the entire estate of which the said CD died possessed is under the value of   pounds as by the annexed inventory may more fully appear, and for the due administration whereof your petitioner is ready and willing to offer a sufficient security.

That your petitioner has no interest antagonistic to the interest of the said infants.

May it therefore please the Probate Officer to appoint your petitioner guardian of said infants and grant him letters of

see over

109

administration of the estate of said deceased as of a person dying intestate, for the use and benefit of said infants.

The said AB makes oath and says that the contents of the foregoing petition are true as therein set forth to the best of deponent's knowledge, information and belief.

Signed

Sworn, &c.

No. 32

AFFIDAVIT VERIFYING INDORSEMENT OF SUMMONS

The High Court/The Circuit Court
In the matter of an Intended Action
In the Estate of XY Deceased
Between AB .... Plaintiff
and CD ..... Defendant

I, AB of   in the county of   [*Description*]
aged 18 years and upwards, the plaintiff in the action about to
be instituted in this matter, make oath and say as follows:

1. I have read the indorsement on the summons intended to be
    issued herein and I say that [*recite here the facts as set out
    in the general indorsement of claim*] and that I am the
    executor [*or as the case may be*] of the last will
    dated the   day of   19   , of the said XY.

2. The said summons is intended to be issued against CD who
    is a lawful son and as such one of the next of kin of the said
    deceased [*or as the case may be*], and because
    he has entered a caveat.

    Signed

    Sworn,&c.

No. 33.

CONSENT TO SET ASIDE CAVEAT

[Heading as in Form No. 1].

In the Estate of XY late of   , deceased
Whereas the above-named XY died on the   day of
19   , having previously made his last will on the   day of
              19

And whereas on the   day of   19   , a Caveat
was entered by Messrs. AB., Solicitors of
for and on behalf of CD the widow of the deceased having
interest

And whereas on the   day of   19   , a Warning
to the said Caveat was lodged by Messrs. EF, Solicitors of
              for and on behalf of GH the sole executor named in the
said will

And whereas on the   day of   19   , an Appearance
to the said Warning was entered by the said AB for and on
behalf of the said CD.

And whereas no contentious proceedings have been
instituted herein

Now it is hereby agreed and consented by, and between,
the said CD and the said GH, as testified by their signatures
and the signatures of their respective solicitors hereunto
subscribed, that the said Caveat, Warning and Appearance to
the said Warning be set aside and that this consent be filed in
the Probate Office.

Signed by the said
in the presence of:

No. 34

RECEIPT FOR LEGACY

Re: deceased.

I,   , hereby acknowledge receipt of a cheque for £200 from   , Executor of the Will of the above-named deceased, per Messrs.   , Solicitors, in full payment of a legacy to me under her said Will in the following terms:

"The sum of two hundred pounds (£200) to
of   County   for her own use and benefit
absolutely"

and I hereby indemnify the said Executor against any claims, demands, costs and expenses howsoever arising, on account of the said payment to me.

Dated:
Signed:
Address:

No. 35

RIGHT OF APPROPRIATION NOTIFICATION

In the estate of   deceased

To: W
     of:

We, AB and CD being the Personal Representatives of the above deceased (hereinafter called "the deceased") late of who died on the day of   19

HEREBY give you notice, pursuant to Section 56 of the Succession Act, 1965 (hereinafter called "the Act") as follows:

1.   You are entitled to require us to appropriate to you under Section 55 of the Act, in or towards satisfaction of any share of the estate to which you are entitled the dwelling in which at the time of the deceased's death, you were ordinarily resident, and also any household chattels.

2.   If your share of the estate is insufficient to enable an appropriation to be made as aforesaid, the right conferred on you may also be exercised in relation to the share of any infant for whom you are a Trustee under Section 57 of the Act, or otherwise.

3.   The Right of appropriation conferred on you as aforesaid shall not be exercisable by you after the expiration of six months from the receipt by you of this notification, or one year from the first taking out of representation of the deceased's estate (which occurred on the   day of   19   ) whichever is the later.

4.   You are required to notify us in writing to appropriate the dwelling under Section 55 of the Act.

Dated:
Signed:

NOTIFICATION OF RIGHT OF ELECTION
WHERE DECEASED SPOUSE DIES WHOLLY TESTATE

In the estate of   deceased

To: W

   of:

We, AB and CD being the Personal Representatives of the above deceased (hereinafter called "the deceased") late of who died on the day of 19 HEREBY give you notice, pursuant to Section 115 of the Succession Act, 1965 (hereinafter called "the Act") as follows:

1. By his last Will [*and Codicil*] dated the   day of   19   the deceased devised and bequeathed to you certain property in the following terms:

[*Here quote from Will*]

The foregoing devise and bequest was not expressed to be in addition to your legal right share under the Act.

2. You may elect to take under Section 115 of the Act, either the property devised and bequeathed to you as aforesaid, or the share to which you are entitled as a legal right.

3. In default of election you will be entitled to take under the Will, and you shall not be entitled to take any share as a legal right.

4   The right of election conferred on you as aforesaid shall not be exercisable after the expiration of six months from the receipt by you of this notification or one year from the first taking out of representation to the deceased's estate (which occurred on the   day of   19   ), whichever is the later.

   Dated:

   Signed:

NOTIFICATION OF RIGHT OF ELECTION
WHERE DECEASED SPOUSE DIES PARTLY TESTATE

In the estate of   deceased.

To: W
      of

We, AB and CD, being the personal representatives of the above deceased (hereinafter called "the deceased") late of   who died on the   day of   19   HEREBY give you notice, pursuant to Section 115 of the Succession Act, 1965 (hereinafter called "the Act") as follows:

1.   Same as 1. in Form No. 36.

2.   The deceased died Intestate in respect of the following property:
[*Here itemise the property, and state its value*]. You are entitled to [all, *one third*] of such property.

3.   You may elect to take, under Section 115 of the Act, either:
    (a) Your share as a legal right under the Act.
    (b) Your share of the property in respect of which the deceased died Intestate, together with the property devised and bequeathed to you as aforesaid.

4.   In default of election you will be entitled to take your share of the property in respect of which the deceased died Intestate, together with the property so devised and bequeathed to you by the Will, but you shall not be entitled to take any share as a legal right.

5.   The same as 4, in Form No. 36.

Dated:
Signed:

ASSENT

Precedent form for use in connection
with the transmission of unregistered land

Shortened Form of Assent (containing minimum requirements only) by single representative in favour of a person absolutely entitled free from incumbrances.

I, AB of   the personal representative of
CD late of   deceased hereby assent to the
vesting in XY of   All that [*here follows
description of property*] [*for all the estate and interest of the
said CD therein at the time of his death*] [*for an estate in fee
simple*].

As witness my hand this   day of   19   .

Signed, etc.

No. 39

Shortened Form of Memorial of an Assent

To the Registrar of Deeds in Ireland.

A Memorial of an Assent made the   day of   19
in relation to the estate of AB late of   deceased
whereby CD   of   and EF
of the said AB assented to the vesting in XY of [*All that etc.*]
[*for an estate in fee simple*] [*for all the estate and interest of the
said AB therein*].

Which said Assent and this Memorial as to the execution
thereof by the said CD are witnessed by   and
                    and which said Assent as to the execution
thereof by the said EF is witnessed by
                              and

Signed and sealed etc.

INDEX